Embracing Affordable Housing:
A Guide to Serving with Heart and God

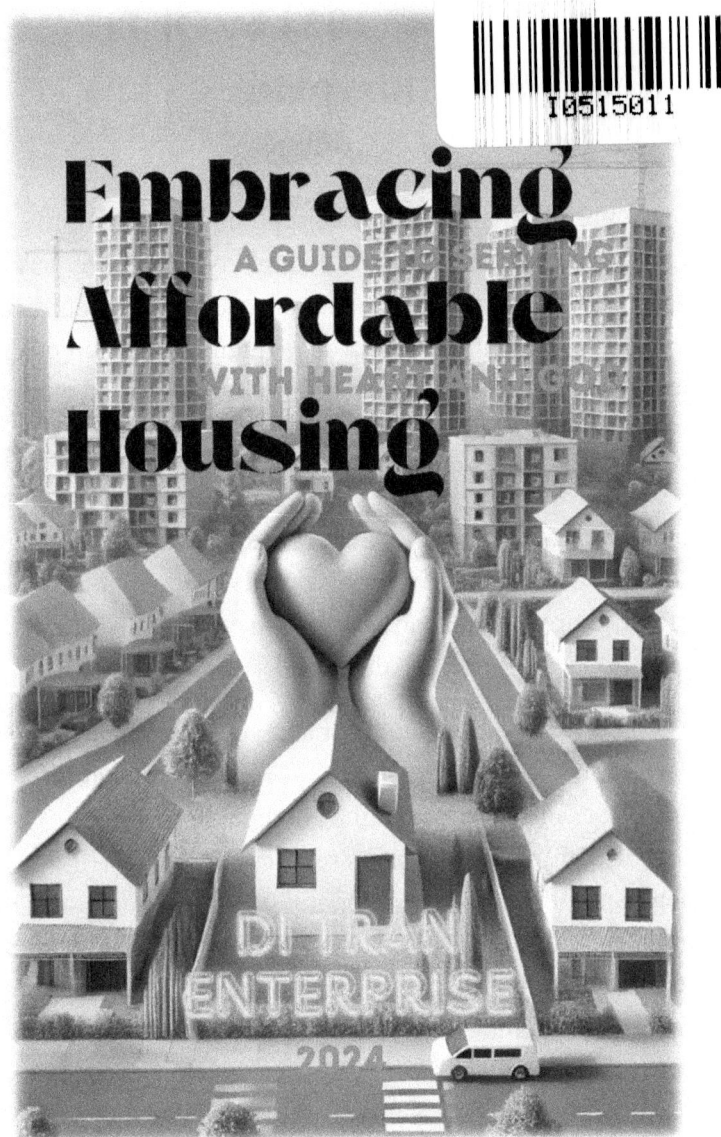

**Embracing Affordable Housing:
A Guide to Serving with Heart and God**

Copyright © 2024 by Di Tran Enterprise

All rights reserved.

No part of this book may be reproduced, stored in a retrieval system, or transmitted in any form or by any means—electronic, mechanical, photocopying, recording, or otherwise—without the prior written permission of the publisher, except for the use of brief quotations in a book review or scholarly journal.

The content provided in this book is intended solely for educational and motivational purposes. It is not intended to serve as a substitute for professional advice. Should you require professional advice, please consult a qualified professional.

The publisher and the author make no representations or warranties with respect to the accuracy, applicability, fitness, or completeness of the contents of this book. They disclaim any warranties (expressed or implied), merchantability, or fitness for any particular purpose. The publisher and the author shall in no event be held liable for any loss or other damages, including but not limited to special, incidental, consequential, or other damages. The views expressed are those of the author alone and should not be taken as expert advice.

Embracing Affordable Housing:
A Guide to Serving with Heart and God

The information in this book is provided "as is," and when you use this information, you do so at your own risk. The contents of this book are intended to provide helpful and accurate information regarding the topics discussed. The publisher and author are not liable for the use or misuse of any materials or information contained in this book.

While every attempt has been made to verify the information provided in this publication, neither the author nor the publisher assumes any responsibility for errors, omissions, or contradictory information contained in this book. Any perceived slights of specific persons, peoples, or organizations are unintentional.

**Embracing Affordable Housing:
A Guide to Serving with Heart and God**

Contents

Copyright © 2024 by Di Tran Enterprise 2

Introduction: Di Tran – A Vietnamese-Born, American-Made Story 6

Chapter 1: Understanding Affordable Housing 12

Chapter 2: Providing Affordable Housing: Practical Strategies and Considerations 23

Chapter 3: Applying for Affordable Housing: Navigating the System and Securing a Home 35

Chapter 4: Affordable Housing as a Business: Blending Profit with Purpose 48

Chapter 5: Infusing Heart and God-Serving Principles into Affordable Housing 62

Chapter 6: Serving Specific Populations: Tailoring Affordable Housing for Unique Needs 76

Chapter 7: Navigating and Mastering the Affordable Housing System 91

Chapter 8: Di Tran Enterprise: Leading with Love, Transparency, and Real Solutions 103

Chapter 9: The Pros and Cons of Affordable Housing as a Business 115

POEM: In Service, We Stand 128

THE END 130

Embracing Affordable Housing:
A Guide to Serving with Heart and God

THANK YOU 130

**Embracing Affordable Housing:
A Guide to Serving with Heart and God**

Introduction: Di Tran – A Vietnamese-Born, American-Made Story

I am Di Tran, a proud American with deep roots in the rich but challenging soil of Vietnam. My story began in a small village, where life was as simple as it was harsh. I was born in a mud hut, where survival was a daily struggle. My father, a man of unyielding strength, owned only one pair of pants, and our meals often consisted of whatever roots we could find to stave off hunger. This was the Vietnam I knew—a place where every day was a battle, and every small victory was cherished.

At the age of six, my life took a significant turn when my mother, driven by her faith and dreams for a better future, sent me to live with Catholic nuns at a boarding school. She envisioned a life where I would serve others, perhaps even as a priest, dedicating myself to the community. From a young age, I learned the value of hard work and discipline. My mother made sure I was busy every day, whether it was attending school, helping at the flea market, or managing tasks in our small businesses. I handled cash transactions, negotiated deals, and interacted with people—essential skills for anyone, but especially challenging for an introverted child like me.

Embracing Affordable Housing:
A Guide to Serving with Heart and God

Despite these experiences, my introverted nature persisted, something I would later confront and learn to embrace. It wasn't until much later in life that I began to understand the true driving force behind everything I did—love. I realized that love is not just an emotion but a fundamental energy that we all possess. It is in front of us, within us, and flows through us. Yet, it often takes silence and self-reflection to recognize this powerful force.

Now, at 42, I see life with a clarity that eluded me in my younger years. Some might call it a midlife crisis or a moment of awakening, but for me, it is an awareness of the profound truth that love is the foundation of everything. Growing up, I was focused on survival, on making something out of nothing. I hustled endlessly, driven by a desire to achieve, to provide, and to succeed. But underneath it all, it was love that propelled me forward—the love for my family, my community, and the future I wanted to build.

Life started with small, humble desires: a piece of bread to eat, a sweet treat to enjoy, or a rare bowl of rice. As my circumstances improved, so did my aspirations. From having a simple meal to sharing it with my family, from providing for my loved ones to expanding that care to my extended family and community, my life's purpose grew alongside my capacity to love. I went from being a child who scavenged for roots to feed his family to becoming a serial small business owner, an educator, a motivational

Embracing Affordable Housing:
A Guide to Serving with Heart and God

speaker, a college professor, and a workforce development advocate in America.

My journey has been one of growth and transformation, fueled by love in all its forms. As a business owner, I have learned that success is not just about profit but about creating value and making a difference in the lives of others. In education, I have discovered the joy of helping others achieve their potential, of seeing graduates walk across the stage and knowing that their future is brighter because of the opportunities I have helped create. As a motivational speaker, I share my story not to boast but to inspire others to find their own path, to believe in their ability to overcome adversity and achieve greatness.

But none of this would have been possible without the understanding that love is the key to everything. It is what connects us, binds us, and drives us to be better. In my work, in my family, in my community, I see the impact of love every day. It is in the smiles of the people I help, in the success of the businesses I build, and in the relationships I nurture.

Today, I am more aware than ever of the importance of being present, of giving without expecting anything in return, and of living with purpose. Whether it's picking up the phone to comfort someone in need, offering a kind word, or simply being there for my children with a smile or

Embracing Affordable Housing:
A Guide to Serving with Heart and God

a kiss, I understand that these small acts of love are what truly matter.

In business, I strive to lead with love, to create environments where people can thrive and feel valued. Whether I am working on a new venture, teaching a class, or mentoring a young entrepreneur, I do so with the knowledge that love is the foundation of all success. It is what makes us human, what gives our lives meaning, and what drives us to achieve our highest potential.

As a father, I am deeply committed to raising my children with the same values that have guided me throughout my life. I want them to know that love is not just something you feel but something you do. It is in the way you treat others, in the way you approach your work, and in the way you live your life. I want them to grow up understanding that true success is not measured by wealth or status but by the impact you have on the lives of others.

Reflecting on my journey, I am filled with gratitude for the challenges I have faced and the lessons I have learned. From the mud hut in Vietnam to the opportunities I have found in America, my life has been a testament to the power of love. It has been the force that has driven me to overcome obstacles, to build a life of meaning and purpose, and to make a difference in the world.

Affordable housing is particularly important to me and is one of the most significant aspects of my story. Growing up

Embracing Affordable Housing:
A Guide to Serving with Heart and God

in Vietnam, I understand what it means to have nothing—to be on the edge of survival. Homelessness in the United States, as challenging as it is, is a situation far better than the life I knew in that mud hut, where we often had nothing to eat. Here, even the homeless have access to food and support from city and state programs, whereas in my homeland, there was no one to care for us.

I remember one night, after a long day of work at Humana as a software engineer, I visited one of my investment properties in downtown Louisville, on Bardstown Road. My experience with these properties always included the challenge of homeless individuals occupying the building—something I didn't mind, but I knew it wasn't sustainable. On that particular night, I encountered a group of young homeless people, aged 20 to 30, rushing out of the building as I arrived. Instead of reacting with frustration, I called out to them, inviting them to join me for dinner. I wanted to learn about their lives, to hear their stories.

What struck me the most that night was a dirty diaper left behind in the building. At that moment, I was reminded of my own children, safe and cared for under a warm roof, while other children were on the streets, vulnerable and exposed to the elements. This realization stayed with me and fueled my passion for affordable housing. I am driven by the knowledge that in this heaven on earth, we must do more to ensure that no child, no person, is left without a place to call home.

Embracing Affordable Housing:
A Guide to Serving with Heart and God

I am Di Tran, Vietnamese-born and American-made. I believe that love is the most powerful force in the universe. It is the key to success, the foundation of happiness, and the driving force behind everything we do. As I continue on this journey, I am committed to living with love, to sharing it with others, and to building a future where love is at the heart of everything we do—especially in the mission to provide affordable housing for all.

**Embracing Affordable Housing:
A Guide to Serving with Heart and God**

Chapter 1: Understanding Affordable Housing

Affordable housing is a term that is often heard in discussions about urban development, community planning, and social welfare. Yet, despite its frequent use, the concept of affordable housing is widely misunderstood. For many, it conjures up images of dilapidated buildings in neglected neighborhoods, associated with poverty and social issues. Others may think of it as a distinct category of housing that is somehow separate from the rest of the market. These misconceptions have created confusion about what affordable housing truly is and why it is so vital to the health and stability of our communities.

In this chapter, we will explore the true nature of affordable housing, clarifying what it is, how it functions, and why it matters. We will break down the misconceptions surrounding affordable housing and reveal the critical role that government programs play in making it accessible to those who need it most. By understanding the reality of affordable housing, we can begin to appreciate its importance and work towards creating solutions that ensure everyone has a safe, decent place to call home.

Defining Affordable Housing

At its core, affordable housing is not a specific type of housing or a separate category of real estate. Rather, it is a

Embracing Affordable Housing:
A Guide to Serving with Heart and God

financial concept—a measure of whether or not a household can afford to pay for housing without compromising their ability to meet other basic needs, such as food, healthcare, transportation, and education. Housing is generally considered affordable when a household spends no more than 30% of its income on housing costs, including rent or mortgage payments, utilities, and other associated expenses.

This 30% threshold is significant because it represents a balance between the need for shelter and the need for other essentials. When housing costs exceed this threshold, families are often forced to make difficult choices, such as cutting back on groceries, skipping medical appointments, or forgoing education opportunities for their children. This is why affordable housing is so crucial—it allows families to maintain a stable and healthy life without sacrificing their basic needs.

But what does affordable housing look like in practice? It can take many forms, from single-family homes to apartments, from urban developments to rural communities. What unites these various forms of housing is not their physical characteristics but the fact that they are made affordable through a combination of market mechanisms and government interventions.

Affordable housing is often provided through rental properties, where the rent is set at a level that is affordable

Embracing Affordable Housing:
A Guide to Serving with Heart and God

for low- to moderate-income families. This can include both privately owned buildings where rents are kept low through government subsidies and publicly owned housing developments operated by local housing authorities. In some cases, affordable housing may also include homeownership opportunities, where the purchase price of a home is subsidized to make it accessible to lower-income buyers.

The Role of Government in Affordable Housing

One of the key aspects of affordable housing is the role that government plays in making it accessible. While the private market is responsible for building and maintaining most housing, the government intervenes to ensure that there is a sufficient supply of affordable housing for those who cannot afford market-rate prices. This intervention takes many forms, including direct subsidies, tax incentives, and regulations designed to protect renters and homeowners.

At the federal level, programs such as the **Housing Choice Voucher Program** (often referred to as Section 8) provide subsidies that help low-income families pay for housing in the private market. These vouchers cover the difference between what a household can afford to pay (based on their income) and the actual rent for the property. This allows families to live in a wider range of neighborhoods, including areas with better schools, job opportunities, and services.

Embracing Affordable Housing:
A Guide to Serving with Heart and God

Another significant federal program is the **Low-Income Housing Tax Credit (LIHTC)**, which incentivizes private developers to build or rehabilitate affordable rental housing. By providing tax credits that reduce the overall cost of development, the LIHTC encourages the creation of housing that is affordable to low-income tenants. This program has been one of the most successful tools for increasing the supply of affordable rental housing in the United States.

State and local governments also play a critical role in affordable housing. They often administer federal programs and provide additional funding and resources to support affordable housing initiatives. This can include direct funding for the construction of new affordable housing units, grants and loans for homebuyers, and support for community-based organizations that provide housing services.

In addition to these financial tools, state and local governments also regulate the housing market through zoning laws, building codes, and tenant protections. These regulations can have a significant impact on the availability and affordability of housing. For example, zoning laws that allow for higher-density development can increase the supply of housing, helping to keep prices in check. On the other hand, restrictive zoning that limits the types of housing that can be built can contribute to housing shortages and drive up prices.

Embracing Affordable Housing:
A Guide to Serving with Heart and God

Local governments are often at the forefront of efforts to address affordable housing challenges. Many cities and towns have established their own affordable housing programs, which may include rent control measures, inclusionary zoning (requiring developers to include affordable units in new projects), and support for non-profit housing developers. These initiatives are often tailored to the specific needs and conditions of the local community, making them an essential part of the overall affordable housing strategy.

The Confusion Unveiled

Despite the critical importance of affordable housing, there is a great deal of confusion about what it actually is and how it functions. This confusion often stems from a lack of understanding of the role that government plays in making housing affordable, as well as misconceptions about who benefits from affordable housing programs.

One of the most common misconceptions is that affordable housing is synonymous with public housing. **Public housing** is a specific type of affordable housing that is owned and operated by the government, typically through local housing authorities. While public housing is an important part of the affordable housing landscape, it represents only a small portion of the overall affordable housing market. The majority of affordable housing is provided through the private market, with government

Embracing Affordable Housing:
A Guide to Serving with Heart and God

support helping to make it accessible to low-income families.

Another misconception is that affordable housing is only for the very poor or for those who are unemployed. In reality, affordable housing serves a wide range of people, including working families, seniors on fixed incomes, veterans, and individuals with disabilities. Many of the people who benefit from affordable housing are employed, often in essential jobs such as teaching, healthcare, and public safety. These individuals contribute to their communities in meaningful ways, yet they may struggle to afford housing in high-cost areas.

Affordable housing is also sometimes misunderstood as a permanent solution, when in fact, it often serves as a temporary support for families and individuals who are working to improve their financial situation. For example, a family may use a housing voucher to afford a safe and stable home while they save for a down payment on a house or work towards a better-paying job. In this way, affordable housing can be a stepping stone to greater financial independence and long-term stability.

Another area of confusion is the role of government subsidies in affordable housing. Some people believe that government assistance is a form of charity or a handout, but in reality, it is a critical part of making the housing market function effectively. Housing is a basic need, and without

Embracing Affordable Housing:
A Guide to Serving with Heart and God

government intervention, many families would be priced out of the market entirely. These subsidies are not about giving something for nothing; they are about ensuring that everyone has the opportunity to live in a safe and decent home, regardless of their income level.

The importance of government assistance in affordable housing cannot be overstated. Without programs like housing vouchers, tax credits, and direct subsidies, the supply of affordable housing would be drastically reduced, leaving millions of families without access to safe, stable housing. Government intervention helps to level the playing field, ensuring that low- and moderate-income families have the same opportunities as others to live in decent housing in communities of their choice.

Government Assistance: The Backbone of Affordable Housing

One of the key aspects of affordable housing that is often overlooked is the role of government assistance in making it possible. Without government support, most affordable housing projects would not be financially viable. This is because the cost of building and maintaining housing is often higher than what low-income families can afford to pay in rent. Government subsidies help to bridge this gap, making it possible to provide housing that is affordable to those who need it most.

Embracing Affordable Housing:
A Guide to Serving with Heart and God

Federal programs like **Section 8 vouchers** and the **Low-Income Housing Tax Credit** (LIHTC) are essential tools in the affordable housing toolkit. Section 8 vouchers provide direct subsidies to low-income families, helping them to afford rent in the private market. The LIHTC, on the other hand, provides tax incentives to developers, encouraging them to build or rehabilitate affordable housing units.

These programs are complemented by state and local initiatives that provide additional funding and support for affordable housing. For example, many states have their own housing finance agencies that provide loans, grants, and tax credits to support affordable housing development. Local governments may also offer incentives to developers, such as reduced permit fees or expedited approval processes, to encourage the construction of affordable housing.

In addition to these financial tools, government agencies also play a critical role in regulating the housing market to ensure that it is fair and accessible. This includes enforcing laws that protect tenants from discrimination, ensuring that housing is safe and habitable, and promoting policies that increase the supply of affordable housing.

Government assistance is not just about providing financial support; it is also about creating the conditions for a healthy and vibrant housing market. By supporting affordable

Embracing Affordable Housing:
A Guide to Serving with Heart and God

housing, the government helps to ensure that communities are diverse and inclusive, with housing options available for people of all income levels. This, in turn, contributes to the overall health and stability of the community, making it a better place to live for everyone.

Ensuring Access to Safe and Decent Housing

At the heart of the affordable housing discussion is the belief that everyone deserves a safe, decent place to live. Housing is a basic human need, and without it, people cannot thrive. This is why affordable housing is so important—it provides the foundation for a stable and healthy life.

Affordable housing ensures that low-income families can access the same quality of housing as those with higher incomes. This is not just about providing shelter; it is about creating environments where people can live with dignity, safety, and hope for the future. Affordable housing is about giving families the opportunity to live in neighborhoods with good schools, access to jobs, and a strong sense of community.

Ensuring access to affordable housing is not just a matter of economics; it is a matter of social justice. When housing is unaffordable, it creates a cycle of poverty and exclusion that is difficult to break. Families who are forced to spend too much of their income on housing often struggle to

Embracing Affordable Housing:
A Guide to Serving with Heart and God

afford other essentials, leading to poor health, lower educational outcomes, and reduced economic opportunities.

Affordable housing breaks this cycle by providing families with the stability they need to build better lives. It gives children a safe place to grow up, free from the stress and instability that comes with housing insecurity. It allows parents to focus on their jobs and their families, rather than worrying about how they will pay the rent. And it strengthens communities by ensuring that everyone, regardless of income, has the opportunity to live in a safe and supportive environment.

Conclusion

Understanding affordable housing requires us to move beyond the misconceptions and recognize the critical role that it plays in our communities. It is not just about providing shelter; it is about ensuring that everyone has the opportunity to live a stable, healthy, and fulfilling life. Affordable housing is supported by a complex web of government programs and initiatives that work together to make housing accessible to those who need it most.

By demystifying the concept of affordable housing and understanding the reality behind it, we can better appreciate its importance and advocate for the policies and programs that support it. Affordable housing is not a handout; it is a necessary intervention that ensures the well-being of individuals, families, and communities. As we move

Embracing Affordable Housing:
A Guide to Serving with Heart and God

forward, it is crucial that we continue to support and expand these programs, ensuring that everyone has access to safe, decent, and affordable housing.

Embracing Affordable Housing:
A Guide to Serving with Heart and God

Chapter 2: Providing Affordable Housing: Practical Strategies and Considerations

Affordable housing is not just a concept; it's a vital necessity for millions of people across the United States. However, the challenge of providing affordable housing is multifaceted and complex. It requires a deep understanding of the economic, social, and regulatory landscape, as well as a commitment to serving the needs of the community. In this chapter, we'll delve into the practical strategies and considerations for developing and maintaining affordable housing. We'll explore the roles of various stakeholders, from private developers to government entities, and discuss the importance of creating housing that is not only affordable but also sustainable and supportive of the broader community.

Understanding the Demand: Identifying the Need

The first step in providing affordable housing is to understand where the need is greatest. This involves conducting thorough market research to identify the demographics that are most in need of affordable housing. These populations typically include low-income families,

Embracing Affordable Housing:
A Guide to Serving with Heart and God

the elderly, veterans, individuals with disabilities, and single-parent households, among others.

To effectively identify the need, developers and policymakers must consider several key factors:

1. **Income Levels:** Understanding the income distribution within a community is critical. By analyzing median income levels and comparing them to local housing costs, it's possible to determine the percentage of households that are cost-burdened (spending more than 30% of their income on housing).

2. **Population Trends:** Demographic trends, such as population growth, aging populations, and migration patterns, can significantly impact the demand for affordable housing. For instance, a growing population of seniors may increase the need for affordable senior housing, while an influx of immigrants may create demand for housing that is both affordable and culturally appropriate.

3. **Existing Housing Stock:** Assessing the current availability of affordable housing within a community helps to identify gaps and areas where additional units are needed. This includes analyzing vacancy rates, the condition of existing housing, and the affordability of both rental and ownership options.

**Embracing Affordable Housing:
A Guide to Serving with Heart and God**

4. **Local Economic Conditions:** The strength of the local economy plays a crucial role in determining housing needs. Areas with high unemployment rates or low wages often have a greater need for affordable housing, as residents struggle to keep up with rising housing costs.

By thoroughly understanding the local demand, developers and policymakers can make informed decisions about where to focus their efforts and how to allocate resources effectively.

Planning and Development: Building Affordable Housing

Once the need for affordable housing has been identified, the next step is to develop a plan for building it. This process involves several stages, from site selection to financing and construction, each of which requires careful consideration and strategic planning.

1. Site Selection: Choosing the right location is one of the most critical decisions in the development process. The ideal site for affordable housing should offer residents access to essential services and amenities, such as public transportation, schools, healthcare, and employment opportunities. Additionally, the site should be located in an area that is safe and free from environmental hazards.

Embracing Affordable Housing:
A Guide to Serving with Heart and God

When selecting a site, developers must also consider zoning laws and land use regulations. Zoning laws can either facilitate or hinder the development of affordable housing, depending on the restrictions they impose. In some cases, developers may need to work with local governments to rezone a property or secure variances that allow for higher-density development.

2. Design and Sustainability: The design of affordable housing is another crucial aspect that impacts both its functionality and its appeal to residents. Good design should prioritize the comfort and well-being of residents, offering units that are well-sized, well-lit, and equipped with modern amenities.

Sustainability is also an essential consideration in the design process. By incorporating energy-efficient building materials and systems, developers can reduce the environmental impact of their projects while also lowering utility costs for residents. Green building practices, such as the use of solar panels, high-efficiency HVAC systems, and water-saving fixtures, can contribute to the long-term affordability of the housing.

3. Financing: Financing is often the most challenging aspect of developing affordable housing. Given that the revenue generated from affordable housing is typically lower than that from market-rate housing, securing sufficient funding can be difficult. However, there are

Embracing Affordable Housing: A Guide to Serving with Heart and God

several financial tools and programs available to support the development of affordable housing:

- **Low-Income Housing Tax Credits (LIHTC):** As mentioned in the previous chapter, LIHTC is one of the most important sources of funding for affordable housing in the United States. This program provides tax credits to developers who agree to set aside a portion of their units for low-income tenants.

- **Community Development Block Grants (CDBG):** Administered by the U.S. Department of Housing and Urban Development (HUD), CDBG funds can be used to finance a wide range of community development activities, including affordable housing.

- **State and Local Programs:** Many states and municipalities offer their own funding programs to support affordable housing. These may include grants, loans, tax incentives, and other forms of financial assistance.

- **Private Financing:** In addition to public funding, developers often rely on private financing to complete their projects. This can include loans from banks, investment from private equity firms, and partnerships with non-profit organizations.

Embracing Affordable Housing:
A Guide to Serving with Heart and God

4. Construction and Development: The construction phase is where the vision for affordable housing becomes a reality. However, this phase is not without its challenges. Developers must manage the construction process carefully to ensure that the project stays on time and within budget. This requires close coordination with contractors, suppliers, and government agencies to address any issues that arise during construction.

Quality control is also essential to ensure that the finished product meets the standards for safety, durability, and livability. Regular inspections and oversight are necessary to identify and address any deficiencies in the construction process.

Maintaining Affordability: Long-Term Strategies

Once affordable housing has been developed, it is essential to ensure that it remains affordable over the long term. This involves several strategies aimed at maintaining affordability while also preserving the quality of the housing and supporting the well-being of residents.

1. Rent Controls and Subsidies: One of the most direct ways to maintain affordability is through rent controls and subsidies. Rent control laws limit the amount by which landlords can increase rent each year, helping to keep housing costs stable for tenants. Meanwhile, subsidies such as Section 8 vouchers provide ongoing financial assistance to help low-income tenants pay their rent.

Embracing Affordable Housing:
A Guide to Serving with Heart and God

2. Property Management: Effective property management is crucial to maintaining the quality and affordability of housing. This includes regular maintenance and repairs, as well as ensuring that the property is safe and clean. Good property management also involves building strong relationships with tenants, addressing their concerns promptly, and fostering a sense of community.

3. Resident Services: Affordable housing is about more than just providing a roof over someone's head; it's about creating a supportive environment where residents can thrive. Many affordable housing developments offer resident services that help tenants improve their financial stability, access healthcare, and pursue education and employment opportunities. These services are an important part of maintaining affordability, as they help residents build the skills and resources they need to achieve long-term stability.

4. Preservation and Rehabilitation: Over time, the condition of affordable housing can deteriorate, making it less desirable and potentially leading to disinvestment. To prevent this, it is essential to invest in the preservation and rehabilitation of affordable housing. This can include renovating existing units, upgrading building systems, and making improvements to common areas and outdoor spaces. Preservation efforts help to ensure that affordable housing remains a viable option for future generations.

Embracing Affordable Housing:
A Guide to Serving with Heart and God

The Role of Partnerships: Collaborating for Success

Providing affordable housing is a complex challenge that requires collaboration among a wide range of stakeholders. Successful affordable housing projects often involve partnerships between government agencies, non-profit organizations, private developers, and community groups. Each of these partners brings unique resources and expertise to the table, making it possible to address the many facets of affordable housing development.

1. Government Partnerships: Government agencies play a crucial role in affordable housing, providing funding, regulatory support, and oversight. By partnering with federal, state, and local governments, developers can access the resources they need to bring their projects to fruition. Government partnerships also help to ensure that affordable housing developments comply with zoning laws, building codes, and other regulations.

2. Non-Profit Organizations: Non-profit organizations are often at the forefront of affordable housing efforts, advocating for policies that support affordable housing and providing direct services to residents. These organizations can be valuable partners in the development process, offering expertise in community engagement, resident services, and property management. Non-profits may also provide funding or act as intermediaries between developers and government agencies.

Embracing Affordable Housing:
A Guide to Serving with Heart and God

3. Private Developers: Private developers bring essential skills and resources to affordable housing projects, including experience in construction, financing, and project management. By partnering with non-profits and government agencies, private developers can leverage public funding and tax credits to make affordable housing projects financially viable. These partnerships also allow private developers to contribute to the social good while still achieving their business goals.

4. Community Engagement: Engaging the community is a critical component of any successful affordable housing project. By involving residents, local businesses, and community leaders in the planning and development process, developers can build support for their projects and ensure that the housing meets the needs of the people it is intended to serve. Community engagement also helps to build trust and foster a sense of ownership among residents, which can contribute to the long-term success of the development.

Overcoming Challenges: Navigating Obstacles in Affordable Housing Development

Despite the many benefits of affordable housing, the development process is not without its challenges. Developers often face significant obstacles, from funding shortfalls to regulatory hurdles, that can delay or derail their projects. However, with careful planning and a

Embracing Affordable Housing:
A Guide to Serving with Heart and God

commitment to collaboration, these challenges can be overcome.

1. Navigating Regulatory Challenges: Zoning laws, building codes, and other regulations can pose significant challenges to affordable housing development. In some cases, developers may need to work with local governments to secure variances or rezone properties to allow for higher-density development. Advocacy and public education can also play a role in addressing regulatory challenges, helping to build support for more flexible and inclusive housing policies.

2. Addressing Funding Gaps: Securing adequate funding is often the most difficult part of developing affordable housing. In addition to pursuing traditional funding sources, developers may need to explore alternative financing options, such as social impact bonds, community land trusts, or public-private partnerships. Creative financing strategies can help to bridge funding gaps and make affordable housing projects financially viable.

3. Building Community Support: Resistance from the community can be a significant barrier to affordable housing development. Concerns about property values, increased traffic, and changes to neighborhood character can lead to opposition from local residents. To address these concerns, developers must engage in transparent and inclusive community engagement efforts, working to build

Embracing Affordable Housing:
A Guide to Serving with Heart and God

trust and demonstrate the benefits of affordable housing for the entire community.

4. Ensuring Long-Term Viability: Finally, developers must plan for the long-term viability of affordable housing projects. This includes not only maintaining the physical condition of the housing but also ensuring that it remains affordable and accessible to those who need it most. Long-term planning should consider potential changes in the housing market, economic conditions, and community needs, with a focus on sustainability and resilience.

Conclusion: Moving Forward with Affordable Housing

Providing affordable housing is both a challenge and an opportunity. It is a challenge because it requires navigating a complex landscape of regulations, funding, and community dynamics. But it is also an opportunity—an opportunity to make a real difference in the lives of individuals and families, to build stronger and more inclusive communities, and to contribute to the social good.

By understanding the practical strategies and considerations involved in affordable housing development, we can move forward with confidence and purpose. Whether you are a developer, policymaker, non-profit leader, or community advocate, your efforts are essential to ensuring that everyone has access to safe, decent, and affordable housing.

Embracing Affordable Housing:
A Guide to Serving with Heart and God

As we continue this journey, let us remember that affordable housing is not just about bricks and mortar—it is about people. It is about creating environments where people can live with dignity, stability, and hope for the future. By working together, we can overcome the challenges and seize the opportunities, building a brighter future for all.

Embracing Affordable Housing:
A Guide to Serving with Heart and God

Chapter 3: Applying for Affordable Housing: Navigating the System and Securing a Home

For many families and individuals, applying for affordable housing can seem like an overwhelming and confusing process. The system is often complex, with multiple programs, agencies, and requirements that vary by location and type of housing. However, understanding the process and being prepared can make a significant difference in securing a safe, stable, and affordable home.

In this chapter, we will break down the steps involved in applying for affordable housing. We'll explore the qualifications required, the application process, and what to expect during the waiting period. By the end of this chapter, you will have a clear roadmap to help you navigate the system and improve your chances of securing affordable housing.

Understanding Eligibility: Who Qualifies for Affordable Housing?

Before you begin the application process, it's important to understand whether you qualify for affordable housing. Eligibility is typically determined by a combination of factors, including income, family size, and citizenship status. While specific requirements may vary depending on the program or housing authority, the following criteria are commonly used to assess eligibility:

1. Income Limits: Income is the most critical factor in determining eligibility for affordable housing. Most affordable housing programs use income limits to ensure that assistance is provided to those who need it most. These limits are usually based on the area median income (AMI) and are adjusted for family size.

For example:

- **Extremely Low-Income:** Households earning 30% or less of the AMI.
- **Very Low-Income:** Households earning 50% or less of the AMI.
- **Low-Income:** Households earning 80% or less of the AMI.

Income limits vary by location, so it's essential to check the specific limits for your area. Some programs, such as Section 8, also consider factors like assets and other sources of income when determining eligibility.

2. Family Size and Composition: The size and composition of your household can also impact your eligibility for affordable housing. Larger families may qualify for higher income limits, and some programs prioritize families with children, elderly members, or

Embracing Affordable Housing:
A Guide to Serving with Heart and God

individuals with disabilities. It's important to provide accurate information about your household when applying, as this will determine the size and type of housing for which you qualify.

3. Citizenship and Immigration Status: Many affordable housing programs require applicants to be U.S. citizens or eligible non-citizens. Eligible non-citizens typically include lawful permanent residents (green card holders), refugees, and individuals granted asylum. Some programs may also serve mixed-status families, where at least one member is a citizen or eligible non-citizen.

4. Residency Requirements: Some affordable housing programs have residency requirements, meaning you must live or work in a specific area to qualify. This is particularly common in local or state-administered programs, which may prioritize applicants who already have ties to the community.

5. Other Criteria: In addition to income and family composition, other factors may be considered when determining eligibility. These can include criminal history, rental history, and creditworthiness. While past issues may not necessarily disqualify you, they can affect your application, so it's important to be upfront and address any potential concerns.

The Application Process: Step-by-Step

Embracing Affordable Housing:
A Guide to Serving with Heart and God

Once you have determined that you meet the eligibility criteria, the next step is to begin the application process. This process can vary depending on the program or housing authority, but the following steps are generally involved:

1. Research and Choose Your Program: The first step in applying for affordable housing is to research the available programs in your area. This includes federal programs like Section 8, state and local housing authorities, and non-profit organizations that offer affordable housing. Each program may have different eligibility criteria, application processes, and waiting lists, so it's important to choose the program that best fits your needs.

- **Section 8 Housing Choice Voucher Program:** One of the most widely known programs, Section 8 provides vouchers that can be used to pay for housing in the private market. The program is administered by local public housing authorities (PHAs), and each PHA has its own application process and waiting list.

- **Public Housing:** Public housing units are owned and managed by local PHAs and offer affordable rental options for low-income families, the elderly, and individuals with disabilities. Unlike Section 8 vouchers, public housing is specific to certain properties.

Embracing Affordable Housing:
A Guide to Serving with Heart and God

- **LIHTC Properties:** Low-Income Housing Tax Credit (LIHTC) properties are privately owned developments that offer affordable rents to qualifying tenants. The application process for these properties is typically handled directly by the property management company.

- **State and Local Programs:** Many states and municipalities offer their own affordable housing programs, which may include rental assistance, homeownership programs, and housing for specific populations such as veterans or seniors.

2. Gather Required Documentation: Before you begin your application, it's essential to gather all the necessary documentation. This may include:

- Proof of income (pay stubs, tax returns, Social Security benefits, etc.)

- Identification (driver's license, passport, Social Security card)

- Birth certificates for all household members

- Proof of citizenship or eligible immigration status

- Documentation of any assets (bank statements, retirement accounts)

- Rental history (lease agreements, rent receipts, landlord references)

Embracing Affordable Housing:
A Guide to Serving with Heart and God

- Background information (criminal history, credit report)

Having these documents ready will help ensure a smooth application process and prevent delays.

3. Submit Your Application: Once you have chosen your program and gathered your documentation, you are ready to submit your application. The application process may vary depending on the program:

- **Online Applications:** Many housing authorities and programs offer online applications, which can be convenient and allow you to track the status of your application.

- **In-Person Applications:** Some programs require you to apply in person at the housing authority office or property management company. This may involve filling out a paper application and submitting your documentation in person.

- **Mail-In Applications:** In some cases, you may be able to submit your application by mail. Be sure to include all required documentation and follow the instructions carefully to avoid any delays.

After submitting your application, it's important to keep a copy for your records and note any confirmation numbers or reference IDs provided.

**Embracing Affordable Housing:
A Guide to Serving with Heart and God**

4. Wait for Confirmation and Next Steps: After submitting your application, you may receive confirmation that your application has been received. This confirmation may include information about the next steps, such as interviews, additional documentation requests, or placement on a waiting list.

5. Participate in Interviews or Additional Screenings: Some programs require applicants to participate in an interview or additional screenings as part of the application process. This may include:

- **Income Verification:** Housing authorities may verify your income by contacting your employer or requesting additional documentation.

- **Background Check:** Some programs conduct background checks to ensure that applicants meet eligibility criteria related to criminal history or creditworthiness.

- **Housing Authority Interview:** You may be required to attend an interview with the housing authority or property management company to discuss your application and verify your information.

It's important to respond promptly to any requests for additional information or interviews, as delays could affect your application status.

Embracing Affordable Housing:
A Guide to Serving with Heart and God

The Waiting Process: Patience and Persistence

After completing the application process, one of the most challenging aspects of securing affordable housing is the waiting period. Due to high demand and limited availability, many affordable housing programs have long waiting lists. Understanding the waiting process and knowing how to navigate it can help you stay on track while you wait for housing to become available.

1. Understanding Waiting Lists: When you apply for affordable housing, you are often placed on a waiting list. The length of time you will spend on the waiting list depends on several factors, including:

- **Demand:** High-demand areas with limited housing options tend to have longer waiting lists.

- **Priority Status:** Some applicants may receive priority placement on the waiting list based on factors such as homelessness, disability, or displacement due to natural disasters.

- **Lottery System:** Some programs use a lottery system to randomly select applicants for placement on the waiting list.

Waiting lists can range from a few months to several years, so it's important to be patient and persistent.

Embracing Affordable Housing:
A Guide to Serving with Heart and God

2. Maintaining Your Place on the Waiting List: While you are on the waiting list, it's essential to maintain your eligibility and keep your application up to date. This may include:

- **Updating Your Information:** Notify the housing authority or property management company of any changes to your income, family size, or contact information.

- **Responding to Inquiries:** Be sure to respond promptly to any inquiries from the housing authority or property management company. Failure to do so could result in your removal from the waiting list.

- **Renewing Your Application:** Some programs require you to renew your application periodically to remain on the waiting list. Be sure to follow the instructions provided to avoid losing your place.

3. Exploring Other Options: While you wait for affordable housing to become available, it's a good idea to explore other options that may be available to you. This could include:

- **Temporary Housing:** Consider seeking temporary housing options, such as staying with family or friends, while you wait for affordable housing.

Embracing Affordable Housing:
A Guide to Serving with Heart and God

- **Applying to Multiple Programs:** Apply to multiple affordable housing programs or properties to increase your chances of securing a home.

- **Housing Assistance Programs:** Explore other housing assistance programs, such as emergency rental assistance, that may provide temporary relief while you wait.

4. Preparing for Move-In: Once you reach the top of the waiting list, you will be contacted by the housing authority or property management company to begin the move-in process. This may include:

- **Finalizing Your Lease:** Review and sign your lease agreement, which will outline the terms and conditions of your tenancy, including rent, security deposit, and maintenance responsibilities.

- **Move-In Inspection:** Participate in a move-in inspection to document the condition of the unit before you move in. This is important for protecting your security deposit and ensuring that any necessary repairs are made before you take possession of the unit.

- **Arranging Utilities:** Set up utility services, such as electricity, gas, and water, in your name before moving in. Be sure to ask the property management company about any utility costs that may be included in your rent.

- **Preparing Your Finances:** Make sure you have the funds available to cover your first month's rent, security deposit, and any other move-in expenses.

Tips for Success: Navigating the Affordable Housing System

Navigating the affordable housing system can be challenging, but there are several strategies you can use to increase your chances of success:

1. Stay Organized: Keep track of all the programs you've applied to, including contact information, application dates, and confirmation numbers. Create a calendar to remind yourself of important deadlines, such as renewal dates or interview appointments.

2. Be Persistent: The affordable housing process can be lengthy and frustrating, but persistence is key. Follow up regularly with housing authorities and property management companies to check on the status of your application and ensure that you remain on the waiting list.

3. Seek Assistance: If you're having trouble navigating the application process, consider seeking assistance from a housing counselor, non-profit organization, or legal aid service. These organizations can help you understand your

Embracing Affordable Housing:
A Guide to Serving with Heart and God

rights, complete your application, and advocate on your behalf.

4. Be Flexible: If possible, be open to considering different housing options, locations, or programs. Expanding your search can increase your chances of finding affordable housing more quickly.

5. Educate Yourself: Stay informed about the affordable housing programs in your area and any changes to eligibility criteria, application processes, or funding availability. This knowledge can help you make informed decisions and stay ahead of the curve.

Conclusion

Applying for affordable housing is a process that requires patience, persistence, and careful planning. By understanding the eligibility criteria, navigating the application process, and preparing for the waiting period, you can increase your chances of securing a safe, stable, and affordable home. Remember that you are not alone—there are resources and organizations available to support you throughout the process.

As you move forward, stay focused on your goal and remain committed to finding the housing that best meets your needs. Affordable housing is more than just a place to live; it's a foundation for a better future. By navigating the system with confidence and determination, you can secure

Embracing Affordable Housing:
A Guide to Serving with Heart and God

the home you deserve and take the first step towards a brighter tomorrow.

Chapter 4: Affordable Housing as a Business: Blending Profit with Purpose

Affordable housing is often viewed solely through the lens of social responsibility, but it is also a viable business model that can be both profitable and impactful. The idea that business success and social good are mutually exclusive is a misconception that this chapter aims to dispel. In reality, affordable housing offers unique opportunities for investors, developers, and entrepreneurs who are committed to creating value while addressing critical societal needs.

In this chapter, we will explore the business side of affordable housing, examining the strategies and considerations involved in making it a sustainable and profitable enterprise. We'll look at how to balance profitability with social impact, the importance of ethical practices, and the role of innovation in driving success in the affordable housing sector.

The Business of Affordable Housing: An Overview

At its core, the business of affordable housing operates on the same principles as any other business: it involves the creation and exchange of value. However, what sets it apart is the dual focus on generating financial returns while also

Embracing Affordable Housing:
A Guide to Serving with Heart and God

meeting a critical social need. This dual mission requires a unique approach, combining traditional business strategies with a deep commitment to social responsibility.

1. Understanding the Market: The affordable housing market is vast and diverse, encompassing a wide range of housing types, income levels, and geographic locations. To succeed in this market, it's essential to understand the specific needs of the target population and the dynamics of the local housing market.

For example, the demand for affordable housing may be higher in urban areas where housing costs have risen sharply, pricing out low- and moderate-income families. Conversely, rural areas may have different challenges, such as limited access to financing or lower availability of land. Understanding these dynamics is crucial for identifying opportunities and making informed business decisions.

2. Identifying Opportunities: One of the key aspects of any successful business is identifying and capitalizing on opportunities. In the affordable housing sector, these opportunities often arise from market gaps, such as unmet demand for housing in specific income brackets or geographic areas.

For example, there may be a shortage of affordable senior housing in a particular community, or a lack of affordable rental units for families. By identifying these gaps, developers can target their efforts to create housing that

Embracing Affordable Housing:
A Guide to Serving with Heart and God

meets the specific needs of underserved populations, thereby maximizing both social impact and financial returns.

3. Revenue Streams: Affordable housing businesses can generate revenue through several streams, including rental income, property sales, and government subsidies. The key is to develop a business model that leverages these revenue streams in a way that is both sustainable and profitable.

- **Rental Income:** For properties developed as affordable rental housing, rental income is the primary revenue stream. While rents are typically lower than market rates, stable occupancy and long-term leases can provide a reliable income stream. Additionally, properties may qualify for rental assistance programs like Section 8, which can supplement tenant payments and ensure consistent cash flow.

- **Property Sales:** In some cases, affordable housing developers may choose to sell units rather than rent them. This can be particularly relevant in affordable homeownership programs, where units are sold at below-market rates to qualifying buyers. The sale of properties can provide a significant upfront return on investment, while also contributing to the long-term financial stability of the business.

**Embracing Affordable Housing:
A Guide to Serving with Heart and God**

- **Government Subsidies and Tax Credits:** Government programs play a critical role in the financial viability of affordable housing projects. Subsidies, grants, and tax credits such as the Low-Income Housing Tax Credit (LIHTC) can offset development costs and enhance profitability. These programs are designed to encourage private investment in affordable housing by reducing financial risk and increasing potential returns.

4. Managing Costs: Managing costs is a fundamental aspect of running a successful affordable housing business. This includes controlling development costs, minimizing operational expenses, and optimizing the use of available resources. Cost management is particularly important in affordable housing, where margins can be thin due to lower rental income and the need to maintain affordability.

Strategies for managing costs may include:

- **Efficient Design and Construction:** Utilizing cost-effective building materials and construction methods can help to keep development costs in check. Modular construction, for example, can reduce both construction time and costs, making it an attractive option for affordable housing projects.

- **Energy Efficiency:** Incorporating energy-efficient systems and materials can reduce long-term operational costs by lowering utility bills for both

Embracing Affordable Housing: A Guide to Serving with Heart and God

the property owner and tenants. These savings can be reinvested into the property or passed on to tenants in the form of lower rents.

- **Leveraging Economies of Scale:** Developing multiple affordable housing projects or larger-scale developments can create economies of scale, reducing per-unit costs and increasing overall profitability. This approach can also provide greater bargaining power with suppliers and contractors.

Balancing Profitability with Social Impact

One of the defining characteristics of affordable housing as a business is the need to balance profitability with social impact. This balance is not only achievable but can also enhance the long-term success of the business. When done right, socially responsible practices can lead to stronger community support, better tenant relations, and a more positive brand reputation—all of which contribute to the bottom line.

1. Ethical Business Practices: Ethical practices are at the heart of balancing profitability with social impact. This means operating with integrity, transparency, and a commitment to the well-being of tenants and the community. Ethical practices in affordable housing might include:

Embracing Affordable Housing:
A Guide to Serving with Heart and God

- **Fair Pricing:** Ensuring that rents or sales prices are truly affordable for the target population, while still allowing for a reasonable return on investment.

- **Quality Construction:** Building housing that is safe, durable, and comfortable, rather than cutting corners to save costs.

- **Tenant Engagement:** Actively involving tenants in decisions that affect their housing, such as property management practices or community improvements.

By prioritizing ethical practices, affordable housing businesses can build trust with tenants, investors, and the community, creating a solid foundation for long-term success.

2. Measuring Social Impact: To effectively balance profitability with social impact, it's important to have a clear understanding of the impact your business is making. This involves setting measurable goals for both financial performance and social outcomes, and regularly assessing progress towards these goals.

For example, a developer might set goals for the number of affordable units created, the number of families housed, or the percentage of tenants who are able to transition to homeownership. By tracking these metrics, the business can demonstrate its impact to stakeholders, attract additional investment, and refine its strategies to achieve even greater results.

3. Engaging with the Community: Community engagement is a key component of balancing profit with purpose. By working closely with local residents, community organizations, and other stakeholders, affordable housing businesses can ensure that their projects meet the needs of the community and contribute to broader social goals.

Community engagement might involve:

- **Listening to Residents:** Holding meetings or focus groups with current and prospective tenants to understand their needs and preferences.

- **Collaborating with Local Organizations:** Partnering with non-profits, community groups, and local governments to provide additional services or amenities that enhance the quality of life for tenants.

- **Supporting Local Economies:** Hiring local workers, using local suppliers, and investing in community development initiatives that benefit the broader neighborhood.

Engaging with the community not only enhances the social impact of affordable housing projects but can also build

Embracing Affordable Housing:
A Guide to Serving with Heart and God

goodwill and reduce opposition to new developments, smoothing the path for future projects.

Innovating for Success: The Role of Technology and Creativity

Innovation is a key driver of success in any business, and affordable housing is no exception. By embracing new technologies, creative approaches, and innovative business models, affordable housing developers can enhance profitability, improve social outcomes, and stay ahead of the competition.

1. Embracing Technology: Technology can play a transformative role in the affordable housing sector, offering new ways to design, build, and manage properties more efficiently and effectively. Some examples of how technology can be leveraged include:

- **Modular and Prefabricated Construction:** These construction methods allow for faster, more cost-effective building, reducing both labor and material costs. Modular units can be manufactured off-site and assembled on-site, speeding up the development process and minimizing disruption to the community.

- **Smart Home Technology:** Incorporating smart home features such as energy-efficient lighting, thermostats, and security systems can enhance the

Embracing Affordable Housing:
A Guide to Serving with Heart and God

appeal of affordable housing while also reducing operational costs. These technologies can also provide added convenience and safety for tenants.

- **Property Management Software:** Advanced property management software can streamline operations, improve tenant communication, and optimize maintenance processes. This can lead to cost savings, better tenant retention, and more efficient use of resources.

2. Creative Financing Models: Innovation in financing is also critical to the success of affordable housing projects. Creative financing models can help bridge funding gaps, reduce risk, and attract additional investment. Some examples include:

- **Social Impact Bonds:** These are performance-based bonds that raise funds for social projects, including affordable housing, with returns linked to the achievement of specific outcomes. This model aligns financial returns with social impact, attracting investors who are motivated by both profit and purpose.

- **Community Land Trusts (CLTs):** CLTs are non-profit organizations that acquire and hold land for the benefit of the community, ensuring that it remains affordable in perpetuity. By separating the ownership of land from the ownership of buildings,

Embracing Affordable Housing:
A Guide to Serving with Heart and God

CLTs can reduce the cost of housing and make it more accessible to low-income families.

- **Public-Private Partnerships (PPPs):** Collaborations between government entities and private developers can provide the resources and expertise needed to deliver large-scale affordable housing projects. PPPs can offer advantages such as shared risk, access to public funding, and streamlined regulatory processes.

3. Developing New Business Models: Innovation in business models can also drive success in the affordable housing sector. For example, some developers are exploring mixed-income developments, where affordable units are integrated with market-rate units. This approach can create more diverse and vibrant communities while also generating additional revenue to support the affordability of the entire project.

Another innovative model is the "micro-unit" concept, which involves building smaller, more affordable units that appeal to single individuals, young professionals, or those looking for a minimalist lifestyle. These units can be more cost-effective to build and maintain, allowing developers to offer lower rents while still achieving profitability.

The Long-Term Vision: Building Sustainable Communities

Embracing Affordable Housing:
A Guide to Serving with Heart and God

The business of affordable housing is not just about creating individual units; it's about building sustainable communities that support the well-being of all residents. This long-term vision requires a commitment to sustainability, social equity, and community development.

1. Sustainable Development: Sustainability is a critical consideration in affordable housing development. This involves not only environmental sustainability but also financial and social sustainability. Sustainable affordable housing projects are those that:

- **Reduce Environmental Impact:** By using energy-efficient materials, renewable energy sources, and sustainable construction practices, developers can minimize the environmental footprint of their projects. This not only benefits the planet but also reduces utility costs for tenants, contributing to long-term affordability.

- **Ensure Financial Viability:** Financial sustainability means that the project can continue to operate and serve residents without requiring ongoing subsidies or facing financial difficulties. This requires careful planning, cost management, and the ability to adapt to changing market conditions.

- **Promote Social Equity:** Social sustainability involves creating housing that is accessible and

Embracing Affordable Housing:
A Guide to Serving with Heart and God

inclusive for all members of the community, regardless of income, race, age, or ability. This includes providing services and amenities that support the health, education, and economic well-being of residents.

2. Supporting Economic Development: Affordable housing can also play a significant role in supporting local economic development. By providing stable, affordable housing, developers can help create a foundation for economic growth, attracting new businesses, and supporting job creation.

Affordable housing developments can also contribute to the revitalization of neighborhoods, bringing new life to areas that may have been neglected or underdeveloped. By investing in community infrastructure, such as parks, schools, and public transportation, developers can enhance the overall quality of life for residents and create more attractive, vibrant communities.

3. Fostering Social Connections: Finally, affordable housing should be designed with the goal of fostering social connections and building a sense of community. This can be achieved through thoughtful design, community engagement, and the provision of shared spaces and amenities.

For example, community centers, gardens, and recreational facilities can provide opportunities for residents to come

Embracing Affordable Housing: A Guide to Serving with Heart and God

together, build relationships, and create a sense of belonging. These social connections are vital for the well-being of residents and can contribute to the long-term success of the community.

Conclusion: Affordable Housing as a Business with Purpose

Affordable housing is more than just a social good; it is a business opportunity that can deliver significant financial returns while also making a meaningful impact on society. By approaching affordable housing with a clear business strategy, a commitment to social responsibility, and a willingness to innovate, developers and entrepreneurs can create successful, sustainable enterprises that benefit both investors and communities.

As we move forward, it's essential to remember that the true measure of success in affordable housing is not just financial profitability but the positive impact we have on the lives of those we serve. By blending profit with purpose, we can build a future where everyone has access to safe, decent, and affordable housing—a future where business and social good go hand in hand.

Embracing Affordable Housing:
A Guide to Serving with Heart and God

Chapter 5: Infusing Heart and God-Serving Principles into Affordable Housing

Affordable housing, at its core, is about more than just providing shelter. It's about creating spaces where people can live with dignity, hope, and a sense of community. In this chapter, we will explore how to integrate heart and God-serving principles into the business of affordable housing. These principles guide us to not only focus on financial success but also to serve with love, compassion, and a deep commitment to the well-being of others. By doing so, we create housing that is not just affordable, but also nurturing, supportive, and aligned with higher values.

The Role of Faith in Business: A Foundation of Service

For many, faith is the bedrock of their values, guiding their decisions, actions, and interactions with others. In the context of affordable housing, faith can provide a powerful framework for service, helping us to see our work not just as a business, but as a calling to serve others in the way that God intended.

1. Serving with a God-Centered Purpose: At the heart of a God-serving approach to affordable housing is the belief that every person is created in the image of God and deserves to live in dignity and safety. This belief compels

Embracing Affordable Housing:
A Guide to Serving with Heart and God

us to serve others with the same love and care that we would wish to receive ourselves. It also reminds us that our work in providing affordable housing is not just about buildings and profits, but about touching lives and making a difference in the world.

Serving with a God-centered purpose means putting people first in all aspects of the business. It means considering how every decision—from the location of a development to the materials used in construction—will impact the lives of the residents. It also means striving to create environments that uplift and empower people, helping them to thrive both physically and spiritually.

2. Embracing the Principles of Humility and Compassion: Jesus' act of washing the feet of His disciples is a powerful example of humility and compassion in service. In the business of affordable housing, these principles can guide us to approach our work with a servant's heart, always seeking to put the needs of others before our own.

Humility in business means recognizing that our role is to serve, not to dominate. It means being open to learning from others, including the very people we are serving. By listening to the needs and concerns of residents, we can create housing that truly meets their needs and reflects their values.

Embracing Affordable Housing:
A Guide to Serving with Heart and God

Compassion, meanwhile, drives us to go beyond the minimum requirements and seek ways to provide more than just basic shelter. It pushes us to think about how we can enhance the quality of life for residents, whether through the design of the housing, the services we provide, or the way we interact with the community.

3. Viewing Profit as a Means, Not an End: In a God-serving business, profit is not the ultimate goal but a means to continue the mission of serving others. Profit allows us to reinvest in our projects, expand our reach, and support more people in need. However, it should never come at the expense of our values or the well-being of those we serve.

This perspective shifts the focus from maximizing profits to maximizing impact. It encourages us to think about how we can use our resources to create the greatest good, whether that means investing in more sustainable building practices, providing additional services for residents, or supporting community initiatives.

Ethical Leadership in Affordable Housing: Guiding with Integrity

Leadership in affordable housing requires more than just business acumen; it requires a strong ethical foundation. Ethical leadership is about making decisions that are not only profitable but also just, fair, and aligned with higher values. It's about setting an example for others to follow

Embracing Affordable Housing:
A Guide to Serving with Heart and God

and building a business that reflects the best of what we believe.

1. Leading with Integrity: Integrity is the cornerstone of ethical leadership. It means being honest and transparent in all our dealings, both with our partners and with the people we serve. In the context of affordable housing, this might involve being upfront about the challenges and limitations of a project, ensuring that all contracts and agreements are fair, and holding ourselves accountable for our actions.

Integrity also means staying true to our mission and values, even when it's difficult. In the competitive world of real estate, there may be temptations to cut corners, inflate costs, or engage in unethical practices to secure a deal or increase profits. Ethical leaders resist these temptations, knowing that true success comes from building a business that is respected and trusted by all.

2. Building Trust and Respect: Trust and respect are essential for any successful business, but they are particularly important in the field of affordable housing, where the stakes are high and the people we serve are often vulnerable. Building trust means being consistent in our actions, keeping our promises, and always acting in the best interests of our residents.

Respect, meanwhile, means recognizing the inherent dignity and worth of every person we serve. It means treating everyone with kindness, fairness, and

Embracing Affordable Housing:
A Guide to Serving with Heart and God

consideration, regardless of their income, background, or circumstances. By building trust and respect, we create a strong foundation for our business and foster positive relationships with residents, partners, and the broader community.

3. Accountability and Stewardship: As leaders in affordable housing, we are stewards of both the resources we manage and the communities we serve. This stewardship carries with it a responsibility to use our resources wisely and to be accountable for the impact of our actions.

Accountability means being open to feedback, willing to admit mistakes, and committed to continuous improvement. It also means being transparent about how we use our resources, whether that's financial capital, land, or human talent. By practicing good stewardship, we ensure that our work has a lasting, positive impact on the communities we serve.

Creating a Culture of Care: Supporting Residents Holistically

Affordable housing is about more than just providing a place to live; it's about creating a supportive environment where residents can thrive. A culture of care is one that prioritizes the well-being of residents, addressing their needs not just as tenants, but as whole people with diverse needs and aspirations.

Embracing Affordable Housing:
A Guide to Serving with Heart and God

1. Providing Holistic Support Services: Holistic support services address the full spectrum of residents' needs, from physical health and safety to mental well-being and economic stability. These services might include:

- **Health and Wellness Programs:** Offering on-site health clinics, mental health services, and wellness programs to support residents' physical and mental health.

- **Economic Empowerment:** Providing job training, financial literacy courses, and employment services to help residents achieve financial stability and independence.

- **Educational Opportunities:** Partnering with local schools, colleges, and non-profits to offer educational programs, tutoring, and scholarships for residents of all ages.

- **Community Building:** Creating spaces and opportunities for residents to connect with one another, such as community centers, gardens, and social events.

By offering holistic support, we help residents not only maintain stable housing but also improve their overall quality of life, empowering them to achieve their goals and contribute to the community.

Embracing Affordable Housing:
A Guide to Serving with Heart and God

2. Designing with Compassion: The design of affordable housing can have a profound impact on residents' well-being. Designing with compassion means creating spaces that are safe, welcoming, and conducive to healthy living. This might involve:

- **Accessibility:** Ensuring that housing is accessible to people with disabilities, including features such as ramps, elevators, and accessible bathrooms.

- **Safety:** Incorporating safety features such as secure entryways, well-lit common areas, and emergency preparedness measures.

- **Comfort:** Designing units that are comfortable and conducive to healthy living, with adequate space, natural light, and ventilation.

- **Community Spaces:** Creating shared spaces where residents can gather, socialize, and build a sense of community, such as gardens, playgrounds, and community rooms.

By designing with compassion, we create environments where residents feel valued and supported, enhancing their overall well-being and sense of belonging.

3. Empowering Residents: Empowerment is a key aspect of a culture of care. Empowering residents means giving them a voice in decisions that affect their lives, supporting

Embracing Affordable Housing: A Guide to Serving with Heart and God

their goals and aspirations, and providing opportunities for them to contribute to the community.

This might involve:

- **Resident Councils:** Establishing resident councils that give tenants a voice in property management decisions, ensuring that their concerns and ideas are heard and addressed.

- **Leadership Opportunities:** Offering leadership development programs and opportunities for residents to take on leadership roles within the community, such as organizing events or leading initiatives.

- **Encouraging Civic Engagement:** Supporting residents in becoming active members of the broader community, whether through volunteering, participating in local government, or advocating for issues that matter to them.

By empowering residents, we help them take ownership of their housing and their community, fostering a sense of pride and responsibility that benefits everyone.

Integrating Faith and Business: A Model for Success

Integrating faith and business is not only possible but can lead to greater success in both realms. When we align our business practices with our spiritual values, we create a

Embracing Affordable Housing:
A Guide to Serving with Heart and God

model that is sustainable, ethical, and impactful. This integration requires intentionality, reflection, and a commitment to continuous growth and improvement.

1. Aligning Business Practices with Spiritual Values: The first step in integrating faith and business is to ensure that our business practices align with our spiritual values. This means reflecting on how our decisions and actions reflect our beliefs, and making adjustments as needed to stay true to our mission.

For example, if our faith calls us to serve the poor and marginalized, we might prioritize projects that serve low-income communities or reinvest a portion of our profits into community development initiatives. If our faith emphasizes the importance of stewardship, we might focus on sustainable building practices and responsible use of resources.

2. Creating a Mission-Driven Organization: A mission-driven organization is one where the mission and values are at the center of everything we do. This means not only setting a clear mission statement but also embedding that mission into the culture, operations, and decision-making processes of the organization.

To create a mission-driven organization, we might:

- **Communicate the Mission:** Ensure that all employees, partners, and stakeholders understand

Embracing Affordable Housing:
A Guide to Serving with Heart and God

and are aligned with the mission and values of the organization.

- **Embed the Mission in Operations:** Integrate the mission into all aspects of the business, from hiring practices to project planning to customer service.

- **Measure Impact:** Regularly assess how well the organization is living up to its mission, using both qualitative and quantitative measures to track progress and identify areas for improvement.

3. Leading with a Servant's Heart: Leading with a servant's heart means putting the needs of others first and serving with humility, compassion, and a commitment to the greater good. This approach to leadership is deeply rooted in many spiritual traditions and can be a powerful force for positive change in the business world.

Servant leadership in affordable housing might involve:

- **Prioritizing the Well-Being of Residents:** Making decisions that prioritize the health, safety, and happiness of residents, even if it means sacrificing short-term profits.

- **Supporting Employees:** Creating a supportive work environment where employees are valued, respected, and given opportunities to grow and develop their skills.

**Embracing Affordable Housing:
A Guide to Serving with Heart and God**

- **Giving Back to the Community:** Using the success of the business to give back to the community, whether through charitable donations, volunteer efforts, or community development projects.

By leading with a servant's heart, we can create a business that is not only successful but also meaningful and fulfilling, both for ourselves and for those we serve.

The Power of Love in Business: Building a Legacy of Care

Love is a powerful force that can transform both individuals and communities. In the business of affordable housing, love means caring deeply about the people we serve and the impact we have on their lives. It means going beyond the minimum requirements and striving to create something truly special, something that will leave a lasting legacy of care.

1. Building Relationships with Residents: At the heart of any successful affordable housing project are the relationships we build with our residents. These relationships are built on trust, respect, and genuine care for their well-being.

Building strong relationships with residents might involve:

- **Regular Communication:** Keeping residents informed and involved in decisions that affect their

Embracing Affordable Housing:
A Guide to Serving with Heart and God

housing, whether through newsletters, meetings, or one-on-one conversations.

- **Responding to Concerns:** Addressing residents' concerns promptly and effectively, showing that we value their input and are committed to their satisfaction.

- **Celebrating Successes:** Recognizing and celebrating the successes and milestones of residents, whether it's a family moving into their first home, a resident finding a new job, or a community coming together for a special event.

2. Creating a Legacy of Care: The legacy we leave behind is not just measured in buildings or profits but in the lives we touch and the communities we build. Creating a legacy of care means ensuring that our impact is lasting, positive, and meaningful.

To create a lasting legacy, we might:

- **Invest in the Long Term:** Focus on creating housing that is not only affordable but also durable, sustainable, and capable of serving future generations.

- **Support Ongoing Community Development:** Continue to support the development of the communities we serve, even after a project is

Embracing Affordable Housing:
A Guide to Serving with Heart and God

completed, by providing resources, services, and advocacy.

- **Mentor the Next Generation:** Share our knowledge, experience, and values with the next generation of affordable housing leaders, helping to ensure that our work continues long into the future.

3. Embracing the Power of Love: Ultimately, the power of love in business is about creating something that goes beyond ourselves, something that reflects the best of who we are and what we believe. It's about using our resources, talents, and opportunities to make the world a better place, one home at a time.

By embracing the power of love, we can create affordable housing that is not just a business, but a ministry—a way to serve God by serving others, to build communities that reflect His love, and to leave a legacy that will inspire and uplift future generations.

Conclusion: A God-Serving Business with Heart

Affordable housing is a unique business opportunity that allows us to blend profit with purpose, creating value not only for ourselves but also for the communities we serve. By integrating heart and God-serving principles into our work, we can build a business that is ethical, impactful, and deeply fulfilling.

Embracing Affordable Housing:
A Guide to Serving with Heart and God

As we move forward, let us remember that our ultimate goal is not just to build houses, but to build homes—places where people feel safe, valued, and loved. By serving with humility, compassion, and a commitment to God's principles, we can create affordable housing that is not just about shelter, but about dignity, hope, and the opportunity for a better life.

This is our mission, our calling, and our legacy. Let us embrace it with all our heart.

**Embracing Affordable Housing:
A Guide to Serving with Heart and God**

Chapter 6: Serving Specific Populations: Tailoring Affordable Housing for Unique Needs

Affordable housing is not a one-size-fits-all solution. Different populations have unique needs that require specialized approaches to ensure that the housing provided is not only affordable but also suitable and supportive. In this chapter, we will explore how to tailor affordable housing solutions for specific populations, including disabled individuals, the elderly, veterans, immigrants, and single parents. We'll discuss the challenges these groups face, the importance of designing housing that meets their needs, and the strategies for providing housing that offers both affordability and dignity.

Housing for Disabled Individuals: Accessibility and Support

Disabled individuals face significant challenges in finding housing that is both affordable and accessible. Many traditional housing units are not designed with the needs of people with disabilities in mind, making it difficult for them to live independently and with dignity. Addressing these challenges requires a focus on accessibility, support services, and a commitment to creating inclusive communities.

Embracing Affordable Housing:
A Guide to Serving with Heart and God

1. Understanding the Needs of Disabled Individuals: Disabled individuals may have a wide range of needs, depending on the nature of their disability. These needs can include physical accessibility, such as wheelchair ramps and wide doorways, as well as features that support individuals with sensory impairments or cognitive disabilities.

When designing housing for disabled individuals, it's essential to consider the following:

- **Mobility:** Ensure that units are designed to accommodate wheelchairs and other mobility aids, with features such as step-free entryways, roll-in showers, and adjustable kitchen counters.

- **Sensory Impairments:** Incorporate features that support individuals with hearing or vision impairments, such as visual alarms, tactile markings, and high-contrast color schemes.

- **Cognitive Disabilities:** Design units that are easy to navigate and minimize sensory overload, with clear signage, simple layouts, and quiet environments.

2. Incorporating Support Services: In addition to accessible design, many disabled individuals require support services to live independently. These services might include:

Embracing Affordable Housing:
A Guide to Serving with Heart and God

- **Personal Care Assistance:** Providing access to personal care aides who can assist with daily activities such as bathing, dressing, and meal preparation.

- **Healthcare Services:** Offering on-site or nearby access to healthcare providers who can manage medical conditions and provide ongoing care.

- **Transportation:** Ensuring that housing is located near accessible public transportation options or providing shuttle services for residents.

By integrating support services into affordable housing for disabled individuals, we can help residents maintain their independence and quality of life.

3. Creating Inclusive Communities: It's important that housing for disabled individuals is integrated into the broader community, rather than being isolated or segregated. Inclusive communities are those where people of all abilities live, work, and interact together, fostering a sense of belonging and mutual respect.

Strategies for creating inclusive communities might include:

- **Mixed-Use Developments:** Developing housing that includes both disabled and non-disabled residents, with shared amenities and spaces that encourage interaction and community building.

Embracing Affordable Housing:
A Guide to Serving with Heart and God

- **Universal Design:** Adopting universal design principles that make housing accessible to everyone, regardless of ability, and reduce the need for specialized modifications.

- **Advocacy and Education:** Working with local governments, businesses, and community organizations to promote awareness and understanding of disability issues, and to advocate for policies that support inclusion.

Housing for the Elderly: Aging in Place with Dignity

The elderly population is one of the fastest-growing demographics in the United States, and many seniors face challenges in finding affordable housing that meets their needs as they age. Providing housing for the elderly requires a focus on safety, accessibility, and services that support aging in place.

1. Designing for Safety and Accessibility: As people age, their physical abilities may decline, making safety and accessibility critical considerations in housing design. Elderly residents are more likely to experience mobility issues, sensory impairments, and chronic health conditions that require special accommodations.

Key design features for elderly housing might include:

Embracing Affordable Housing:
A Guide to Serving with Heart and God

- **Non-Slip Flooring:** Installing non-slip flooring in bathrooms, kitchens, and other areas prone to spills can help prevent falls.

- **Grab Bars and Handrails:** Placing grab bars in bathrooms and handrails in hallways can provide extra support for residents with mobility challenges.

- **Accessible Bathrooms:** Designing bathrooms with walk-in tubs, roll-in showers, and raised toilets can make them more accessible for elderly residents.

- **Easy-to-Use Fixtures:** Installing fixtures such as lever-style door handles, touch-activated faucets, and rocker light switches can make daily tasks easier for seniors.

2. Supporting Aging in Place: Aging in place refers to the ability of seniors to live independently in their own homes for as long as possible. To support aging in place, affordable housing for the elderly should offer a range of services that help residents maintain their independence while receiving the care they need.

These services might include:

- **In-Home Care:** Providing access to home health aides who can assist with activities of daily living, such as bathing, dressing, and medication management.

Embracing Affordable Housing:
A Guide to Serving with Heart and God

- **Meal Services:** Offering meal delivery or communal dining options for residents who may have difficulty preparing their own meals.

- **Transportation:** Ensuring that residents have access to transportation for medical appointments, grocery shopping, and social activities.

- **Social and Recreational Programs:** Organizing social and recreational activities that promote physical and mental well-being, such as exercise classes, arts and crafts, and group outings.

3. Fostering a Sense of Community: For many seniors, social isolation is a significant concern, especially if they live alone or have limited mobility. To combat isolation, it's important to create a sense of community within elderly housing developments.

Strategies for fostering community might include:

- **Community Centers:** Developing on-site community centers where residents can gather for social activities, educational programs, and events.

- **Shared Outdoor Spaces:** Creating gardens, walking paths, and patios where residents can enjoy the outdoors and interact with their neighbors.

- **Intergenerational Programs:** Partnering with local schools, youth organizations, or volunteer groups to

Embracing Affordable Housing:
A Guide to Serving with Heart and God

create intergenerational programs that bring together seniors and younger community members.

Housing for Veterans: Honoring Those Who Served

Veterans face unique challenges when it comes to housing, including physical disabilities, mental health issues, and difficulties transitioning to civilian life. Providing affordable housing for veterans requires a deep understanding of these challenges and a commitment to honoring their service.

1. Addressing Physical and Mental Health Needs: Many veterans have service-related disabilities that require specialized housing and support. These needs might include:

- **Accessible Housing:** Ensuring that housing is fully accessible for veterans with mobility impairments, including features such as wheelchair ramps, wide doorways, and roll-in showers.

- **Mental Health Support:** Providing access to mental health services, including counseling, therapy, and support groups for veterans dealing with conditions such as PTSD, depression, or anxiety.

- **Substance Abuse Treatment:** Offering substance abuse treatment and recovery programs for veterans struggling with addiction.

Embracing Affordable Housing:
A Guide to Serving with Heart and God

2. Supporting the Transition to Civilian Life: The transition from military to civilian life can be challenging for many veterans, particularly when it comes to finding stable housing and employment. Housing for veterans should include support services that help them navigate this transition.

These services might include:

- **Job Training and Placement:** Offering job training programs and employment assistance to help veterans find work in civilian sectors.

- **Financial Counseling:** Providing financial counseling and budgeting assistance to help veterans manage their finances and build financial stability.

- **Peer Support Programs:** Creating peer support groups where veterans can connect with others who have had similar experiences and offer mutual support.

3. Creating a Supportive Community: Veterans often benefit from living in a community where they can connect with others who share their experiences and understand the challenges they face. Creating a supportive community for veterans involves:

Embracing Affordable Housing:
A Guide to Serving with Heart and God

- **Veteran-Specific Housing:** Developing housing specifically for veterans, where they can live among others who have served and share a common bond.

- **Supportive Services on Site:** Offering on-site services such as case management, healthcare, and counseling to provide comprehensive support for veterans.

- **Partnerships with Veteran Organizations:** Collaborating with veteran organizations, such as the VA or local veterans' groups, to provide additional resources and services.

Housing for Immigrants: Supporting New Americans

Immigrants face a unique set of challenges when it comes to housing, including language barriers, cultural differences, and legal obstacles. Providing affordable housing for immigrants requires a focus on accessibility, cultural sensitivity, and support services that help them integrate into their new communities.

1. Addressing Language and Cultural Barriers:
Language and cultural differences can create significant challenges for immigrants when navigating the housing system. To address these barriers, housing providers should:

- **Multilingual Services:** Offer application assistance, leasing information, and support services

Embracing Affordable Housing:
A Guide to Serving with Heart and God

in multiple languages to ensure that immigrants can understand and access the housing options available to them.

- **Cultural Competence Training:** Provide cultural competence training for property managers, staff, and service providers to ensure that they understand and respect the cultural backgrounds of immigrant residents.

- **Culturally Appropriate Design:** Consider cultural preferences when designing housing units and common areas, such as the layout of kitchens or communal spaces that accommodate larger family gatherings.

2. Providing Legal and Social Support: Many immigrants face legal challenges related to their immigration status, which can affect their ability to secure housing. Providing legal and social support can help immigrants navigate these challenges and find stable housing.

These services might include:

- **Legal Assistance:** Offering legal assistance for immigration issues, such as obtaining residency or citizenship, and for housing-related matters, such as eviction defense.

Embracing Affordable Housing:
A Guide to Serving with Heart and God

- **Case Management:** Providing case management services to help immigrants access public benefits, healthcare, education, and employment opportunities.

- **Community Integration Programs:** Developing programs that help immigrants integrate into their new communities, such as language classes, cultural orientation, and mentorship programs.

3. Building Inclusive Communities: Creating inclusive communities where immigrants feel welcome and supported is essential for their long-term success. Strategies for building inclusive communities might include:

- **Community Outreach:** Engaging with immigrant communities through outreach and partnerships with local immigrant organizations to ensure that housing developments meet their needs and reflect their values.

- **Resident Engagement:** Encouraging immigrant residents to participate in community activities, resident councils, and leadership opportunities to build a sense of ownership and belonging.

- **Celebrating Diversity:** Organizing cultural events, festivals, and celebrations that highlight the diversity of the community and bring together residents from different backgrounds.

Embracing Affordable Housing:
A Guide to Serving with Heart and God

Housing for Single Parents: Providing Stability and Support

Single parents face significant challenges in finding affordable housing that provides stability and support for their families. These challenges include financial constraints, childcare responsibilities, and the need for safe, family-friendly environments. Providing affordable housing for single parents requires a focus on creating supportive, family-oriented communities.

1. Offering Family-Friendly Housing: Housing for single parents should be designed with the needs of families in mind, offering units that are spacious, safe, and conducive to family life.

Key features of family-friendly housing might include:

- **Spacious Units:** Providing units with multiple bedrooms, ample storage, and open living areas that accommodate the needs of children.

- **Safety Features:** Ensuring that housing developments have secure entryways, well-lit common areas, and safe outdoor play spaces for children.

- **Child-Friendly Amenities:** Offering amenities such as playgrounds, childcare facilities, and after-school programs that support the needs of families.

Embracing Affordable Housing:
A Guide to Serving with Heart and God

2. Providing Support Services for Single Parents: Single parents often juggle multiple responsibilities, making it difficult to balance work, childcare, and other obligations. Support services can help ease these burdens and provide stability for single-parent families.

These services might include:

- **Childcare Assistance:** Providing on-site childcare services or partnering with local childcare providers to offer affordable childcare options for working parents.

- **Parenting Support:** Offering parenting classes, support groups, and resources for single parents to help them navigate the challenges of raising children on their own.

- **Financial Assistance:** Providing financial counseling, budgeting assistance, and access to public benefits to help single parents manage their finances and achieve financial stability.

3. Creating a Supportive Community: Building a supportive community for single parents involves creating a network of resources, services, and social connections that help them thrive.

Strategies for creating a supportive community might include:

Embracing Affordable Housing:
A Guide to Serving with Heart and God

- **Peer Support Groups:** Establishing peer support groups where single parents can connect with others who share similar experiences and offer mutual support.

- **Resident Engagement:** Encouraging single parents to participate in community activities, leadership opportunities, and decision-making processes to foster a sense of belonging and empowerment.

- **Partnerships with Local Organizations:** Partnering with local schools, non-profits, and community organizations to provide additional resources and services that support single-parent families.

Conclusion: A Commitment to Tailored, Compassionate Housing Solutions

Providing affordable housing for specific populations requires a deep understanding of their unique needs and a commitment to creating tailored, compassionate solutions. Whether it's housing for disabled individuals, the elderly, veterans, immigrants, or single parents, the goal is always the same: to provide safe, affordable, and supportive housing that enhances the quality of life for residents and helps them achieve stability and success.

As we continue to develop and provide affordable housing, let us remember that every resident has a unique story and a unique set of needs. By approaching our work with compassion, cultural sensitivity, and a commitment to service, we can create housing that not only meets basic needs but also uplifts and empowers those we serve.

This is the heart of affordable housing—meeting people where they are, understanding their challenges, and providing solutions that are as diverse and dynamic as the communities we serve. Through our efforts, we can build not just houses, but homes—places where everyone, regardless of their background or circumstances, can live with dignity, hope, and a sense of belonging.

Chapter 7: Navigating and Mastering the Affordable Housing System

In the complex world of affordable housing, success often comes to those who are proactive, informed, and engaged. Whether you are a developer, a policy advocate, or an individual seeking housing, understanding the intricacies of the system is key to achieving your goals. This chapter will delve into the importance of mastering the affordable housing system, providing practical advice on how to navigate its complexities and how to become an effective advocate for change. We will discuss strategies for staying informed, engaging with key stakeholders, and using your

Embracing Affordable Housing: A Guide to Serving with Heart and God

influence to make a positive impact on the affordable housing landscape.

Understanding the Complexity: Why Mastering the System Matters

The affordable housing system is a vast and intricate network of programs, policies, regulations, and stakeholders. It involves multiple levels of government, a range of funding sources, and a variety of housing types and programs. For those involved in affordable housing—whether as providers, advocates, or recipients—it is essential to understand this complexity and how to navigate it effectively.

1. The Role of Government Programs and Policies: Government programs and policies are the backbone of affordable housing. They determine who qualifies for assistance, how funding is allocated, and what types of housing are developed. Key programs like the Low-Income Housing Tax Credit (LIHTC), Section 8 vouchers, and public housing are administered at the federal, state, and local levels, each with its own set of rules and requirements.

Understanding these programs is crucial for anyone involved in affordable housing. For developers, it means knowing how to apply for and manage funding, how to comply with regulations, and how to design projects that meet the needs of the community. For advocates, it means

Embracing Affordable Housing:
A Guide to Serving with Heart and God

understanding how policies are made and how to influence them to better serve those in need. For individuals seeking housing, it means knowing what options are available and how to access them.

2. The Interplay of Market Forces: Affordable housing does not exist in a vacuum; it is deeply influenced by broader market forces, including the availability of land, the cost of construction, and local economic conditions. Housing markets can vary dramatically from one region to another, and what works in one area may not be feasible in another.

To master the affordable housing system, it's essential to understand how these market forces impact housing availability and affordability. This includes knowing how to assess local housing needs, how to identify opportunities for development, and how to navigate the challenges of fluctuating markets. By staying informed about market trends and conditions, you can make better decisions and position yourself for success.

3. The Importance of Collaboration: The complexity of the affordable housing system means that no one can succeed alone. Collaboration is essential—whether it's between developers and government agencies, advocates and community groups, or residents and property managers. Effective collaboration allows for the pooling of

Embracing Affordable Housing:
A Guide to Serving with Heart and God

resources, the sharing of expertise, and the building of strong, supportive networks.

Understanding how to collaborate effectively is a key part of mastering the affordable housing system. This includes knowing how to build partnerships, how to engage with stakeholders, and how to navigate the often-complicated relationships between different entities. By fostering collaboration, you can enhance your impact and achieve better outcomes for those you serve.

Staying Informed: The Power of Knowledge

In the fast-changing world of affordable housing, staying informed is critical. Policies shift, funding streams evolve, and new challenges and opportunities emerge. To navigate the system effectively, you must be committed to continuous learning and staying up-to-date with the latest developments.

1. Keeping Up with Policy Changes: Housing policy is constantly evolving, influenced by changes in government, economic conditions, and societal needs. New laws and regulations can have a profound impact on affordable housing, affecting everything from funding availability to eligibility criteria.

To stay informed, it's important to regularly monitor policy developments at the federal, state, and local levels. This might involve subscribing to industry newsletters, attending

Embracing Affordable Housing:
A Guide to Serving with Heart and God

housing conferences, and participating in webinars and workshops. By staying on top of policy changes, you can anticipate challenges, seize opportunities, and ensure that your work remains aligned with current regulations.

2. Understanding Funding Sources: Funding is the lifeblood of affordable housing, and understanding where to find it and how to access it is essential. This includes not only traditional funding sources like government grants and tax credits but also new and innovative financing models such as social impact bonds and public-private partnerships.

Staying informed about funding opportunities requires regular research and networking. This might involve connecting with housing finance agencies, attending funding workshops, or participating in industry associations. By keeping your finger on the pulse of funding trends, you can ensure that your projects are well-funded and financially sustainable.

3. Engaging with the Community: Staying informed is not just about understanding policies and funding; it's also about staying connected with the communities you serve. This means regularly engaging with residents, listening to their needs and concerns, and staying attuned to the social and economic conditions that affect their lives.

Community engagement can take many forms, from town hall meetings and focus groups to surveys and informal

Embracing Affordable Housing:
A Guide to Serving with Heart and God

conversations. By staying informed about the needs of the community, you can design housing that truly meets their needs and build stronger, more resilient communities.

Engaging with Key Stakeholders: Building Relationships That Matter

Navigating the affordable housing system effectively requires strong relationships with key stakeholders, including government agencies, community organizations, and residents. These relationships are the foundation of successful affordable housing projects and advocacy efforts.

1. Building Relationships with Government Agencies: Government agencies are central to the affordable housing system, overseeing funding, regulations, and policy implementation. Building strong relationships with these agencies is essential for accessing resources, navigating regulatory challenges, and advocating for change.

To build these relationships, it's important to approach government agencies as partners rather than adversaries. This might involve regular communication, participation in public meetings, and collaboration on projects and initiatives. By establishing trust and demonstrating your commitment to the public good, you can build relationships that support your goals and help you navigate the complexities of the system.

**Embracing Affordable Housing:
A Guide to Serving with Heart and God**

2. Collaborating with Community Organizations:
Community organizations play a critical role in affordable housing, providing services, advocacy, and support to residents. These organizations often have deep connections to the communities they serve and can be valuable partners in housing development and advocacy efforts.

Collaboration with community organizations might involve joint projects, shared advocacy efforts, or partnerships on service delivery. It's important to approach these collaborations with a spirit of mutual respect and a commitment to shared goals. By working together, you can amplify your impact and create housing that truly serves the needs of the community.

3. Engaging Residents as Partners: Residents are at the heart of affordable housing, and engaging them as partners is essential for success. This means not only listening to their needs and concerns but also involving them in decision-making processes and empowering them to take an active role in their communities.

Engaging residents might involve establishing resident councils, hosting regular meetings, and providing opportunities for residents to participate in leadership and advocacy roles. By treating residents as partners, you can build trust, foster a sense of ownership, and create stronger, more vibrant communities.

Advocacy and Influence: Making Your Voice Heard

Embracing Affordable Housing:
A Guide to Serving with Heart and God

Effective participation in the affordable housing system requires not only understanding and navigating the system but also advocating for change. Whether you are pushing for policy reforms, advocating for funding, or raising awareness of housing issues, advocacy is a powerful tool for making a positive impact.

1. Understanding the Advocacy Landscape: Advocacy in affordable housing involves a wide range of activities, from lobbying elected officials to organizing community campaigns. Understanding the advocacy landscape means knowing who the key players are, what the key issues are, and how to effectively communicate your message.

To be an effective advocate, it's important to stay informed about the current political climate, the priorities of policymakers, and the needs of the community. This might involve joining advocacy organizations, participating in coalitions, and staying connected with other advocates and stakeholders.

2. Building a Strong Advocacy Network: Advocacy is often most effective when it's done in collaboration with others. Building a strong advocacy network involves connecting with other individuals and organizations who share your goals and working together to amplify your impact.

This might involve forming coalitions, participating in joint campaigns, and sharing resources and expertise. By

Embracing Affordable Housing:
A Guide to Serving with Heart and God

building a strong network, you can increase your influence, reach a broader audience, and achieve greater success in your advocacy efforts.

3. Communicating Your Message Effectively: Effective advocacy requires clear and compelling communication. Whether you're speaking to policymakers, the media, or the public, it's important to articulate your message in a way that resonates with your audience and motivates them to take action.

This might involve developing clear talking points, using data and stories to illustrate your message, and tailoring your communication to different audiences. By communicating your message effectively, you can build support for your cause and drive meaningful change.

The Importance of Proactivity: Staying Ahead of the Curve

In the dynamic world of affordable housing, staying ahead of the curve is essential for success. This means not only reacting to changes as they happen but also anticipating challenges and opportunities and positioning yourself to take advantage of them.

1. Anticipating Challenges: The affordable housing landscape is full of challenges, from funding cuts and regulatory changes to economic downturns and shifting market conditions. Anticipating these challenges means

Embracing Affordable Housing:
A Guide to Serving with Heart and God

staying informed, staying flexible, and being prepared to adapt your strategies as needed.

This might involve conducting regular risk assessments, staying connected with industry experts, and developing contingency plans for potential challenges. By anticipating challenges, you can stay ahead of the curve and position yourself for success even in difficult times.

2. Seizing Opportunities: In addition to challenges, the affordable housing landscape is also full of opportunities. Whether it's a new funding source, a policy change, or a market shift, being proactive means being ready to seize these opportunities as they arise.

To seize opportunities, it's important to stay informed, stay connected, and be ready to act quickly. This might involve staying in regular contact with funding agencies, participating in policy discussions, and staying attuned to market trends. By being proactive, you can take advantage of opportunities and position yourself for success.

3. Continuous Improvement: Finally, staying ahead of the curve requires a commitment to continuous improvement. The affordable housing landscape is constantly evolving, and success requires a willingness to learn, adapt, and grow.

This might involve regularly evaluating your strategies, seeking out new knowledge and skills, and being open to

Embracing Affordable Housing:
A Guide to Serving with Heart and God

feedback and new ideas. By committing to continuous improvement, you can stay at the forefront of the affordable housing field and continue to make a positive impact for years to come.

Conclusion: The Power of Mastery in Affordable Housing

Navigating and mastering the affordable housing system is essential for success in this complex and challenging field. Whether you are a developer, advocate, or individual seeking housing, understanding the intricacies of the system and being proactive in your approach can make all the difference.

By staying informed, engaging with key stakeholders, and being an effective advocate, you can navigate the affordable housing landscape with confidence and achieve your goals. And by being proactive, anticipating challenges, and seizing opportunities, you can position yourself for success and make a meaningful impact on the lives of those you serve.

In the end, mastering the affordable housing system is about more than just navigating complexity; it's about using your knowledge, skills, and influence to create positive change. It's about building a better future for all, where everyone has access to safe, affordable, and dignified housing. And it's about staying true to your

Embracing Affordable Housing:
A Guide to Serving with Heart and God

mission, your values, and your commitment to serving others with heart and integrity.

Embracing Affordable Housing:
A Guide to Serving with Heart and God

Chapter 8: Di Tran Enterprise: Leading with Love, Transparency, and Real Solutions

Di Tran Enterprise stands as a beacon of integrity, compassion, and innovation in the affordable housing sector. Under the leadership of Di Tran, the enterprise has not only made significant strides in providing affordable housing but has also set a new standard for how business can be conducted with heart and purpose. This chapter will delve into the unique approach of Di Tran Enterprise, exploring how it addresses real needs with real solutions, empowers others to enter the affordable housing business, and maintains a steadfast commitment to transparency, clarity, and love in all its endeavors.

A Vision Rooted in Service

From the very beginning, Di Tran Enterprise was founded on a simple yet profound vision: to serve those in need by providing them with the basic dignity of a safe and affordable home. This vision is deeply rooted in Di Tran's personal values and his unwavering belief that every individual deserves a chance to live with dignity, security, and hope.

1. Serving with a Purpose: At the core of Di Tran Enterprise is a purpose-driven mission to address the

Embracing Affordable Housing:
A Guide to Serving with Heart and God

housing crisis by creating real, tangible solutions. This mission goes beyond the mere construction of housing units; it encompasses a holistic approach to community building, economic empowerment, and social equity.

Di Tran's commitment to service is evident in every aspect of the enterprise's work. Whether it's through the development of new housing projects, the rehabilitation of existing properties, or the provision of supportive services, Di Tran Enterprise is dedicated to making a meaningful difference in the lives of those it serves.

2. A Focus on Real Needs: One of the defining characteristics of Di Tran Enterprise is its focus on addressing real needs. This means not only providing housing but also ensuring that the housing meets the specific needs of the residents, whether they are low-income families, the elderly, disabled individuals, or veterans.

To achieve this, Di Tran Enterprise conducts thorough needs assessments for each project, engaging with residents, community leaders, and local organizations to understand the unique challenges and opportunities in the area. This information is then used to design housing that is not only affordable but also accessible, safe, and supportive of the residents' overall well-being.

3. A Commitment to Empowerment: Di Tran Enterprise believes that true service goes beyond providing for

Embracing Affordable Housing:
A Guide to Serving with Heart and God

immediate needs; it involves empowering individuals and communities to achieve long-term stability and success. This philosophy is reflected in the enterprise's approach to affordable housing, which includes not only the provision of housing but also the support and resources needed to help residents thrive.

This commitment to empowerment is evident in the range of services offered by Di Tran Enterprise, from job training and financial counseling to educational programs and community development initiatives. By providing these resources, the enterprise helps residents build the skills and confidence they need to achieve their goals and improve their quality of life.

Transparency and Clarity: Building Trust with Stakeholders

In an industry where trust is paramount, Di Tran Enterprise stands out for its unwavering commitment to transparency and clarity. These principles are not just ideals; they are the foundation of the enterprise's business practices, guiding every decision and interaction with stakeholders.

1. Transparent Operations: Transparency in operations is a hallmark of Di Tran Enterprise. From the initial planning stages of a project to the final implementation, the enterprise ensures that all stakeholders are kept informed and involved in the process. This includes regular updates

Embracing Affordable Housing: A Guide to Serving with Heart and God

on project timelines, budgets, and any challenges that may arise.

Di Tran Enterprise also takes a proactive approach to addressing any concerns or questions from stakeholders, whether they are residents, community members, or investors. By maintaining open lines of communication and providing clear, accurate information, the enterprise builds trust and fosters strong, collaborative relationships.

2. Ethical Financial Practices: Financial transparency is another key aspect of Di Tran Enterprise's approach. The enterprise is committed to ethical financial practices, ensuring that all funds are managed responsibly and that financial reports are accurate and accessible to stakeholders.

This commitment to financial transparency extends to the pricing of housing units as well. Di Tran Enterprise works to ensure that rents are set at levels that are truly affordable for residents, without hidden fees or unexpected increases. This approach not only helps residents maintain financial stability but also builds trust and confidence in the enterprise's commitment to their well-being.

3. Clear Communication: Clarity in communication is essential for building trust and ensuring that all stakeholders are on the same page. Di Tran Enterprise prioritizes clear, honest communication in all its

Embracing Affordable Housing:
A Guide to Serving with Heart and God

interactions, whether it's with residents, partners, or the broader community.

This includes providing clear explanations of project goals, timelines, and expectations, as well as being upfront about any challenges or limitations. By communicating clearly and honestly, Di Tran Enterprise fosters a culture of openness and accountability, where stakeholders feel valued and respected.

Providing Real Solutions to Real Problems

In a world where housing is often treated as a commodity, Di Tran Enterprise takes a different approach—one that focuses on providing real solutions to real problems. This means not only addressing the immediate need for affordable housing but also tackling the underlying issues that contribute to housing instability and insecurity.

1. Innovative Housing Solutions: Di Tran Enterprise is known for its innovative approach to housing development, using creative solutions to address the unique challenges of each project. This might involve using modular construction to reduce costs and construction time, or incorporating sustainable design elements to lower utility bills and improve environmental impact.

The enterprise also explores alternative housing models, such as mixed-income developments or co-housing communities, which offer a more flexible and inclusive

Embracing Affordable Housing:
A Guide to Serving with Heart and God

approach to housing. By thinking outside the box, Di Tran Enterprise is able to create housing that is not only affordable but also sustainable, adaptable, and responsive to the needs of the community.

2. Comprehensive Support Services: Recognizing that housing alone is not enough to ensure stability, Di Tran Enterprise provides a range of comprehensive support services designed to help residents succeed. These services are tailored to the specific needs of the population served and may include:

- **Job Training and Employment Services:** Helping residents develop the skills they need to secure stable, well-paying jobs.

- **Financial Counseling:** Providing guidance on budgeting, saving, and managing debt to help residents achieve financial independence.

- **Health and Wellness Programs:** Offering access to healthcare services, mental health support, and wellness programs to promote overall well-being.

- **Education and Youth Programs:** Supporting the educational needs of residents, particularly children and young adults, to ensure they have the opportunities they need to succeed.

By providing these services, Di Tran Enterprise helps residents build a strong foundation for the future, reducing

Embracing Affordable Housing: A Guide to Serving with Heart and God

the risk of housing instability and creating a path to long-term success.

3. Addressing Systemic Issues: In addition to providing direct services, Di Tran Enterprise is also committed to addressing the systemic issues that contribute to the affordable housing crisis. This involves advocacy for policy changes, collaboration with other organizations, and efforts to raise awareness of the challenges facing low-income communities.

Di Tran Enterprise engages in advocacy at the local, state, and federal levels, pushing for policies that increase funding for affordable housing, protect tenants' rights, and promote fair housing practices. The enterprise also works to build partnerships with other organizations, leveraging collective resources and expertise to tackle the complex, multifaceted issues that contribute to housing insecurity.

Empowering Others: Helping New Entrants into the Affordable Housing Business

Di Tran Enterprise is not only focused on its own success but is also committed to helping others enter the affordable housing business. By sharing knowledge, resources, and expertise, the enterprise empowers new developers, non-profits, and community leaders to create their own impact in the affordable housing sector.

Embracing Affordable Housing:
A Guide to Serving with Heart and God

1. Mentorship and Training Programs: Recognizing the challenges that new entrants face in the affordable housing industry, Di Tran Enterprise offers mentorship and training programs designed to equip them with the skills and knowledge they need to succeed. These programs cover a wide range of topics, from project planning and financing to regulatory compliance and community engagement.

Through these mentorship programs, Di Tran Enterprise provides hands-on guidance, helping new developers navigate the complexities of the industry and avoid common pitfalls. By investing in the next generation of affordable housing leaders, the enterprise ensures that more communities have access to the housing they need.

2. Collaborative Projects: Di Tran Enterprise also collaborates with new entrants on joint projects, providing them with the opportunity to gain experience and build their portfolios. These collaborations are designed to be mutually beneficial, allowing new developers to learn from the enterprise's expertise while contributing fresh ideas and perspectives.

Collaborative projects might involve co-developing a housing complex, partnering on a mixed-use development, or working together on a community revitalization initiative. By working together, Di Tran Enterprise and its partners can achieve greater impact and create more sustainable, inclusive communities.

Embracing Affordable Housing:
A Guide to Serving with Heart and God

3. Providing Access to Resources: One of the biggest barriers for new entrants in the affordable housing sector is access to resources, including funding, land, and technical expertise. Di Tran Enterprise helps to bridge this gap by connecting new developers with the resources they need to bring their projects to life.

This might involve providing introductions to funding sources, offering technical assistance with project planning and design, or helping to navigate the regulatory landscape. By providing access to these resources, Di Tran Enterprise empowers new developers to succeed and contribute to the growth of the affordable housing sector.

Leading with Love: The Heart of Di Tran Enterprise

At the heart of Di Tran Enterprise is a commitment to leading with love. This means approaching every aspect of the business with compassion, empathy, and a deep sense of responsibility to those served. It's about creating housing that is not just affordable but also nurturing, supportive, and reflective of the dignity and worth of every individual.

1. Compassionate Leadership: Di Tran's leadership style is characterized by compassion and a genuine concern for the well-being of others. This compassionate approach is reflected in the enterprise's commitment to listening to the needs of residents, engaging with the community, and providing services that enhance quality of life.

Embracing Affordable Housing:
A Guide to Serving with Heart and God

Compassionate leadership also means creating a positive work environment for employees, where they feel valued, supported, and inspired to do their best work. By leading with compassion, Di Tran sets the tone for the entire organization, fostering a culture of care that extends to every project and every interaction.

2. A Culture of Care: Di Tran Enterprise is committed to creating a culture of care, both within the organization and in the communities it serves. This culture of care is built on the principles of respect, inclusion, and support, ensuring that everyone feels valued and empowered.

In practice, this means creating housing that is designed with the well-being of residents in mind, offering services that support their physical, mental, and emotional health, and fostering a sense of community and belonging. By cultivating a culture of care, Di Tran Enterprise creates environments where people can thrive and reach their full potential.

3. A Legacy of Love: The ultimate goal of Di Tran Enterprise is to leave a legacy of love—one that is defined by the positive impact it has on the lives of those it serves. This legacy is built on the belief that business can be a force for good, creating value not just in financial terms but in human terms.

Di Tran Enterprise's legacy is one of communities transformed, lives improved, and opportunities created. It's

Embracing Affordable Housing:
A Guide to Serving with Heart and God

a legacy that reflects the enterprise's commitment to service, compassion, and the belief that everyone deserves a place to call home.

Conclusion: A Model for the Future

Di Tran Enterprise is more than just a business; it's a model for how affordable housing can be done with integrity, compassion, and purpose. By focusing on real solutions to real problems, leading with transparency and clarity, and empowering others to enter the field, the enterprise has set a new standard for what is possible in the affordable housing sector.

As Di Tran Enterprise continues to grow and expand its impact, it remains committed to its core values and its mission to serve. Whether through the development of new housing projects, the mentorship of new developers, or the provision of comprehensive support services, the enterprise is dedicated to making a positive difference in the lives of those it serves.

In a world where housing is increasingly out of reach for many, Di Tran Enterprise stands as a beacon of hope, showing that with the right approach, it is possible to create housing that is affordable, sustainable, and rooted in love. This is the future of affordable housing—a future where everyone has access to a safe, dignified, and supportive place to call home.

Embracing Affordable Housing:
A Guide to Serving with Heart and God

Embracing Affordable Housing:
A Guide to Serving with Heart and God

Chapter 9: The Pros and Cons of Affordable Housing as a Business

Affordable housing, while often viewed through a lens of social responsibility, is also a viable business model that can generate stable returns for developers, investors, and entrepreneurs. However, it is a complex field, heavily regulated and shaped by a variety of government programs, financing options, and market conditions. Understanding the pros and cons of affordable housing as a business is crucial for anyone considering entering this sector. This chapter will explore the advantages and challenges of affordable housing as a business, with a particular focus on the restrictions and opportunities associated with financing, vouchers, subsidies, and property management.

The Pros of Affordable Housing as a Business

1. **Stable Demand:** Affordable housing is in high demand across the United States, particularly in urban areas where housing costs have skyrocketed. This demand provides a steady market for affordable housing developers and investors, ensuring a consistent stream of tenants and, in turn, stable rental income.

2. **Government Support:** A significant advantage of affordable housing is the availability of government support in the form of subsidies, tax credits, and

Embracing Affordable Housing:
A Guide to Serving with Heart and God

vouchers. Programs like the Low-Income Housing Tax Credit (LIHTC) and Section 8 vouchers provide financial incentives and reduce risk for developers. These programs are designed to encourage private investment in affordable housing by making it more financially viable.

3. **Social Impact:** Beyond financial returns, affordable housing offers the opportunity to make a significant positive impact on communities. Providing safe, stable, and affordable housing helps to alleviate poverty, reduce homelessness, and improve the overall quality of life for low-income families, veterans, and disabled individuals.

4. **Diversification:** For real estate investors, affordable housing can be an attractive way to diversify their portfolios. Because it operates under different market dynamics compared to luxury or market-rate housing, it can provide a buffer against economic downturns, as demand for affordable housing often remains strong even during recessions.

5. **Long-Term Investment:** Affordable housing can be a long-term, stable investment. Properties are often subject to extended affordability periods (sometimes 15 to 30 years), which means they can provide consistent income over a long period. Additionally, the demand for affordable housing is

Embracing Affordable Housing:
A Guide to Serving with Heart and God

unlikely to diminish, making it a reliable investment for the future.

The Cons of Affordable Housing as a Business

1. **Complex Regulations:** Affordable housing is heavily regulated, with complex rules governing everything from tenant eligibility to rent prices. Navigating these regulations can be challenging and requires specialized knowledge. Compliance with government programs like LIHTC, Section 8, or Veterans Affairs Supportive Housing (VASH) vouchers involves significant paperwork and ongoing monitoring, which can be burdensome for developers and property managers.

2. **Financing Restrictions:** Financing for affordable housing projects often comes with strings attached. For example, the LIHTC program requires properties to remain affordable for a specified period (typically 15 to 30 years), during which time the developer cannot sell the property at market rates. These restrictions can limit flexibility and reduce potential profits.

3. **Vouchers and Subsidies Limitations:** While vouchers like Section 8 or VASH provide steady rental income, they also come with limitations. For instance, voucher payments are capped at a certain level, which may be below market rent.

Embracing Affordable Housing: A Guide to Serving with Heart and God

Additionally, the process of qualifying tenants and maintaining compliance with voucher programs can be time-consuming and requires diligent management.

4. **Limited Cash Flow Potential:** Affordable housing projects typically generate lower cash flow compared to market-rate housing due to rent restrictions. While government subsidies and tax credits can help offset these lower rents, the overall profitability of affordable housing may be lower, particularly in the early years of a project.

5. **Market Perception and Stigma:** Affordable housing can sometimes face opposition from local communities, who may associate it with lower property values or increased crime. Overcoming this stigma requires effective community engagement and education, which can add to the complexity of developing affordable housing projects.

6. **Long Holding Periods:** Due to restrictions tied to government programs, affordable housing properties often come with long holding periods, during which they must remain affordable. This can limit an investor's ability to sell or repurpose the property, potentially tying up capital for decades.

**Embracing Affordable Housing:
A Guide to Serving with Heart and God**

Understanding Financing Restrictions and Voucher Programs

Affordable housing projects are often financed through a combination of government programs, private investment, and loans. Understanding the restrictions associated with these financing options is critical for success.

1. **Low-Income Housing Tax Credit (LIHTC):** The LIHTC program is the primary tool for financing affordable housing in the United States. It provides tax credits to developers in exchange for building or rehabilitating affordable housing. However, LIHTC properties are subject to strict affordability requirements, typically for a 15-year compliance period, followed by an extended use period of at least another 15 years.

    - **Affordability Period:** During this time, the property must remain affordable, and rents cannot exceed a certain percentage of tenant income.

    - **Restrictions on Sale:** The property cannot be sold at market value during the affordability period, limiting the owner's ability to capitalize on market appreciation.

    - **Compliance:** Developers must ensure ongoing compliance with LIHTC

Embracing Affordable Housing: A Guide to Serving with Heart and God

regulations, including income verification for tenants and reporting to state agencies.

2. **Section 8 Housing Choice Vouchers:** Section 8 vouchers are a key source of funding for affordable housing, providing rental assistance to low-income families. Tenants pay a portion of their income towards rent, with the voucher covering the remainder.

    - **Rent Restrictions:** Rents for Section 8 units are capped based on fair market rent calculations, which may be lower than market rates in some areas.
    - **Tenant Qualification:** Tenants must meet income eligibility criteria, and property managers must verify income and ensure compliance with HUD regulations.
    - **Project-Based Vouchers:** Unlike tenant-based vouchers, project-based vouchers are tied to specific units within a property. These units must remain affordable for a fixed period, usually 10 to 20 years.

3. **Veterans Affairs Supportive Housing (VASH) Vouchers:** VASH vouchers provide rental assistance specifically for homeless veterans, often

Embracing Affordable Housing:
A Guide to Serving with Heart and God

coupled with case management and supportive services.

- **Veteran Focus:** Properties accepting VASH vouchers must ensure that the units are reserved for veterans and that supportive services are available.
- **Compliance:** Like other voucher programs, VASH requires strict compliance with HUD regulations and ongoing reporting.

4. **Project-Based Vouchers (PBV):** Project-Based Vouchers (PBVs) are similar to Section 8 but are attached to specific properties rather than individual tenants.

   - **Affordability Period:** PBV units must remain affordable for at least 10 to 15 years, during which they cannot be rented at market rates.
   - **Property Requirements:** PBV properties must meet specific HUD standards, including accessibility and safety requirements.
   - **Long-Term Commitment:** Owners must commit to providing affordable housing for the duration of the voucher term, limiting flexibility in managing the property.

**Embracing Affordable Housing:
A Guide to Serving with Heart and God**

Subsidies and How to Obtain Them

Subsidies are a crucial component of affordable housing finance, helping to bridge the gap between the cost of development and the rents that low-income tenants can afford. Understanding how to obtain these subsidies and the restrictions associated with them is essential for developers and investors.

1. **Government Grants:** Various federal, state, and local governments offer grants to support affordable housing development. These grants can be used for construction, rehabilitation, or operating expenses.

    - **Application Process:** Obtaining grants typically involves a competitive application process, requiring detailed proposals and documentation.
    - **Restrictions:** Grants often come with strings attached, such as requirements to maintain affordability for a certain period or to serve specific populations.
    - **Monitoring:** Recipients of government grants are subject to ongoing monitoring and reporting requirements to ensure compliance with grant terms.

2. **Tax Increment Financing (TIF):** TIF is a public financing method that uses future tax revenue

Embracing Affordable Housing:
A Guide to Serving with Heart and God

increases to fund current improvements, such as affordable housing.

- **Eligibility:** TIF is typically available in designated redevelopment areas and requires approval from local government entities.
- **Restrictions:** TIF funds must be used for specific purposes, such as infrastructure improvements or development costs, and are subject to local oversight.
- **Repayment:** Developers may be required to repay TIF funds if project goals, such as job creation or affordable housing targets, are not met.

3. **Home Investment Partnerships Program (HOME):** The HOME program provides federal block grants to states and localities to fund affordable housing projects.

    - **Affordability Requirements:** Properties funded by HOME must remain affordable for a period ranging from 5 to 20 years, depending on the level of assistance provided.
    - **Income Limits:** HOME-funded units must be rented or sold to low-income families, with income limits set by HUD.

Embracing Affordable Housing:
A Guide to Serving with Heart and God

- **Matching Funds:** Developers may be required to provide matching funds or leverage other financing sources to qualify for HOME assistance.

4. **Capital Subsidies:** Capital subsidies are direct payments or financial assistance provided by government agencies to reduce the upfront cost of developing affordable housing.

   - **Funding Sources:** Capital subsidies can come from federal programs like the Community Development Block Grant (CDBG) or state and local housing finance agencies.

   - **Restrictions:** Like other subsidies, capital subsidies often come with long-term affordability requirements and restrictions on how the funds can be used.

   - **Repayment:** In some cases, capital subsidies may be structured as loans that must be repaid if affordability requirements are not met.

Sale or Hold: Managing Properties for Cash Flow

One of the critical decisions in affordable housing is whether to hold or sell properties. This decision is

Embracing Affordable Housing:
A Guide to Serving with Heart and God

influenced by the restrictions tied to financing and subsidies, as well as the investor's long-term strategy.

1. **Holding Properties:** Holding affordable housing properties can provide stable, long-term cash flow, especially when rents are supported by government programs like Section 8 or LIHTC.

    - **Long-Term Income:** Holding properties allows investors to benefit from steady rental income over the long term, which can be particularly attractive in stable markets.

    - **Compliance Obligations:** Holding properties requires ongoing compliance with affordability restrictions and government regulations, which can be resource-intensive.

    - **Asset Appreciation:** Over time, properties may appreciate in value, providing the opportunity for refinancing or leveraging equity for new investments.

2. **Selling Properties:** Selling affordable housing properties can generate a significant return, particularly if the market value has increased. However, selling is often subject to restrictions.

    - **Affordability Periods:** Properties financed through programs like LIHTC are typically subject to extended affordability periods, during which they cannot be sold at market rates.

- **Right of First Refusal:** In some cases, nonprofit partners or government entities may have a right of first refusal, allowing them to purchase the property before it is sold on the open market.

- **Exit Strategies:** Developers must plan exit strategies carefully, considering the potential impact on tenants and the community. Selling properties too soon may result in penalties or the loss of subsidies.

Conclusion: Balancing Profit and Purpose in Affordable Housing

Affordable housing presents both opportunities and challenges as a business. While it offers the potential for stable returns and significant social impact, it is also a complex field with numerous regulations, restrictions, and risks. Success in affordable housing requires a deep understanding of the financial and regulatory landscape, as well as a commitment to balancing profit with purpose.

By carefully navigating the pros and cons, understanding the restrictions and opportunities associated with financing and vouchers, and making informed decisions about

Embracing Affordable Housing:
A Guide to Serving with Heart and God

holding or selling properties, developers and investors can build successful businesses that not only generate income but also contribute to the well-being of communities. In the end, affordable housing is about more than just profit—it's about creating lasting value for society and building a future where everyone has a place to call home.

**Embracing Affordable Housing:
A Guide to Serving with Heart and God**

POEM: In Service, We Stand

In the footsteps of the One who knelt,
To wash the feet of those He held dear,
We too shall bend, our hearts to melt,
In service to all, with love sincere.

In these days of strain, where prices climb,
Where housing's weight is hard to bear,
We build small spaces, just enough,
A sanctuary found in compact care.

Less than five hundred square, they call their own,
Condos or homes in small embrace,
Yet within these walls, love is known,
A community thrives in a gentle space.

With hands that heal, and hearts that care,
The nuns, the nurses, the pharmacy's grace,
Kentucky Pharmacy stands prepared,
In this haven, all find their place.

Di Tran Enterprise, a beacon bright,
In a world where costs bring worry and fear,
We serve each other, day and night,
To build, to grow, and to endear.

We offer work, we offer life,
A cycle of love that knows no end,

Embracing Affordable Housing:
A Guide to Serving with Heart and God

For God loves all, through joy and strife,
And so we serve, each one a friend.

Generations rise, in this sacred bond,
A legacy of care, of hearts entwined,
In this place, our spirits respond,
To the call of love, in service aligned.

So let us wash each other's feet,
In this inflation, where burdens are shared,
For in this service, our hearts will meet,
God's love made real, in lives prepared.

**Embracing Affordable Housing:
A Guide to Serving with Heart and God**

THE END

THANK YOU